POWER MEDITATION

Created By,

Mr Paul J Tavares MSC BSC

Stress Management & Empowerment Instructor
Expert of the Subconscious Mind
NLP & Other Alternative Therapy
Certified Teacher of various Wellbeing Modalities
Dan Grade – In Numerous Martial Art Disciplines

ISBN: 9781075815324
Copywrite © Paul Tavares JUNE 2019

I would like to thank my family, mentors, teachers, peers &
students for encouraging and supporting me in writing this book.
A special thanks to my son Ethan Tavares for all the deep level
mind, body, emotion and spirit discussions we have had. Further
thanks to my wife who has been, as always, extremely supportive
in this process. And a big thank you to Professor Martyn Davis,
for his mentoring and encouragement in publishing my first
book.

What is power meditation? It is a technique you can deploy to
rapidly put yourself in a state of <u>total</u> connection with your inner
and outer world! It is a collection of meditative exercises
designed to offer a quick fix of empowering yet rejuvenating
energy! Life can be pleasurable or a complete nightmare!!

Do you dare to tread the path the universe has set out for you?!? Are you ready to consume every minute of your life with bold attentiveness in the midst of uncertainty? Are you past dreaming? Or can you make a drastic change and become a far-reaching high achiever who will make a profound change in a world that truly needs real hero's?!?!

I have explored many paths in my life and I see myself like a tree with many branches of essential knowledge to offer, much like the one above. Make sure that you grow in a direction that is viable for your life mission, always trust your intuition! This book is filled with revolutionary meditations for a wide range of audiences. They will help you gain the energy to take leaps of faith and stay along your chosen path, come what may. Whoever you are, you WILL find pertinence and substance in this unique compilation. My life mission is to thrust people into states of empowerment! Especially the weak and vulnerable!! I have highlighted many words in bold from here on, so that as you read them, they enrich your mind positively at a subconscious level. Words that stand out stick in the mind! Let **positive** words stick in your mind and your actions never stagnate in the real world! And I hope and PRAY that the words I have highlighted **positively alter** your mind unknowingly, while you read each sentence. With time, you will literally be catapulted into a **positive & idyllic state of mind**!! Life is an opportunity to be yourself and do what makes YOU feel **fulfilled**!! Trust your own voice and not that of the no-hoper who believes in nothing but procrastination!

Believe in yourself! Be the super powerful vertebrate you were created to be, not an insect! Take the bull by the horns! Do all you can to be healthy, strong and make a difference! How can you think anyone else will believe in you if you yourself, don't? Align with whatever path is best for you in a strong awakened state and go with the natural flow of what is meant to be. But do it with your eyes forced wide open! Perhaps the "real you" is a **compilation** of many personas and energies that have positively infected your life. Perhaps all the **heroes** and **heroines** you look/have looked up to in the past have been more influential than the genetic code that fills all the microscopic cells in your body! We become a cocktail of all the influences around us, whether this information comes from books, television.... or real people and experiences. Or perhaps, you believe you are completely unique and set aside from any personality type you have ever seen! Maybe some of you will have had the strength to choose only SPECIFIC traits you have seen in others and embodied them in your persona with no effort at all! Well done to you! Your personality is bound to fluctuate and so too will the way you approach your **positive development** and meditation hereafter. As you evolve and grow, your compilation of beliefs are certain to change. Develop yourself as you read and note down any real experiences you have had through using the meditations I have provided. Always keep an open mind, marvel at the discoveries and triumphs along the way! Developing yourself through deeply connecting with your innermost needs is a huge step to connecting deeply with other people.

When I ask people why they chose to study and learn meditation or any longevity discipline like Yoga, Tai Chi, Chi Gong, martial arts or meditation, the vast majority answer "to **regulate** overthinking and the negative thought processes in my mind." Remember, that the mind is in a constant perpetual state of flux regardless of who you are. The world is in a state of change! So is your mind! How many times do you change your mind!!!? I have been so fortunate to have been able to study numerous ways to calm and settle the mind and emotions. But there is no glory in studying something and not applying it in your life! I have done a lot of work on myself through my training in longevity arts like Tai Chi, Yoga, martial arts, studies of Complimentary Alternative Medicine & other therapy disciplines. The world has so much to offer in the way of self-development and there is always a unique meditative discipline for every single individual in our **enchanting** and diverse world. Calming the mind is good after trauma, but maybe your mind actually needs something substantial to chew on! Give it what it wants and trust your intuition!! Not what someone else tells you it wants! Would you deny your stomach a certain type of food? Then why starve your mind of the true energy it needs? Sometimes the mind must be settled, but you should always consider adding **wakeful expansive energy** as an alternative.

Remember that sometimes you may need the opposite of what everyone else thinks you need! Maybe you need to stir up your mind to experience **awakening**! Today, most people are already in deep meditative states with their eyes open while walking to work and back! Any small change to their routine like standing in a longer than usual queue becomes a terrifying process. Meditations that put a security guard to sleep are going to get him fired or beaten up! While employed in the corporate world, I used specific meditations to enhance my levels of receptivity while taking exams like PRINCE2 & NEBOSH. This book is laced with meditative exercises from the beginning till the end starting on the very next page. Some of the process's hereafter will inject wakeful energy into a practitioner and others will do the opposite! To use this book properly, think about what you really need as a person and apply which meditations are useful. Happy meditating!!

Contemplation meditation – for concentration and insight

Look at the picture below and contemplate the deeper meaning behind it, for you. Stack together as many insights as you can for the next 3 to 5 minutes.

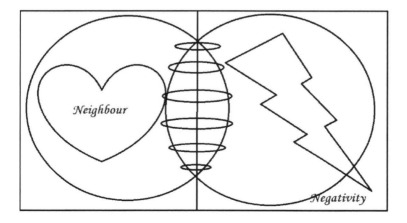

I look at this image in two ways. As a Catholic, I think religiously, of the two statements made by Christ and think of how to apply them to my own life. Jesus Christ said to "cut out what causes you to sin" and to "love your neighbour". For me, this fits perfectly into the yogic and Tai Chi ethos of YinYang and embracing everything around us, so as to be moving slowly in a **positive** direction towards the evolution of a better self. Yoga means unionisation of everything that exists. Not just the mind, body and spirit. The rings overlap from one frame to the next and represent the transition of energy from one form to another. The rings themselves are oval like the loops of energy common in our universe. Planets orbit stars, moons orbit planets, convection currents circle in a room and electrons orbit protons & neutrons in atoms. Circles are symbols of power in many ancient cultures. When they overlap like a "venn diagram" energy can **flow** through distinct paths. What did the representation above reveal to you?

Let this book diminish the illusion of happiness through selfish acquisition in the material world. **Happiness** through gain of material possession or wealth will never last, because material possessions themselves perish! Our powerful blue, green and white planet moves energy through cycles. Water moves in cycles; carbon cycles and even human beings recycle their creations. Everything rots and is recycled in the end, even at the **macroscopic level** a blue star has a finite life cycle. There is no true past, present or future, these are merely human concepts. Actions sit forever in the stream of time, so make sure yours carry **virtuous** energy! Like attracts like and hate attracts hate! If you are already in a positive state of mind, you can further elevate your level of positivity energetically by adding positive affirmations into all your daily routines.

You can say affirmations first thing in the morning, or if you have commitments first thing, say them any time of the day, but make sure you do. Positive self-talk is essential for a **compassionate**, **strong** and trouble-**free** state of mind.

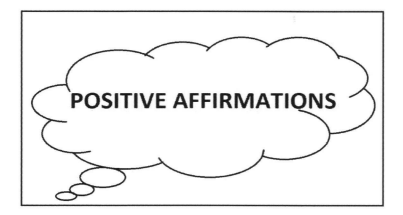

Positive affirmations will help you create the life you want. You won't know unless you actually **try**! Affirmations don't always work instantly. If you have a nasty bacterial disease, how long do you take an antibiotic? For long enough for it to work! The same rule applies to affirmations! You must remember not to completely cut out negative emotions, these are prompts from within to change a particular behaviour. Behaviour that is negative that brings about a negative emotion or temporarily masks a negative feeling should be rooted out and understood before it gets out of hand. You should also note that what is negative for you may not necessarily be negative for someone else. The person who blocked your drive may have had to exit in an emergency to reach in time and save a life! I will reveal strategies from successful philosophies used by ancient cultures that really work to **infuse positivity** into a troubled mind. These **techniques** are ones that have withstood the test of time itself.

What I mean by this, is that the techniques I speak of, are still being used by highly **successful** people in this day and age! If they have lasted for so long, surely you should value them! I hope you do! I hope you value information and learning that relates to wellness because these commodities are priceless!

Become that single person who **positively** stands out from those all around you in situations where many will crumble under pressure! A simple yet powerful affirmation you can use as a daily mantra right now could be **"I create positive habits all the time".** Perhaps you need to make a decision now, to work on being one of those people who works well inside and outside of pressure. The world certainly needs more people like this. While everyone is in panic and disarray, you will be quite the opposite, if you work through the meditations **habitually**. You will be the **hero** if you deploy the tools given to you in this book! The tools within will continue to **empower** you and give you true strength, courage and the willpower to persist. Let these very words and sentences empower you each time you read through. I have tested the techniques in many of my clients and students. They really work!! Of course, there will be times that will really challenge you and you may not even want to try. But you will have a more powerful and highly evolved mindset that is better able to deal with those serious events and challenges. And you will take **big leaps** into places others dare not to tread. You will face your demons with the sparkle of a true master in your eyes and become the person you were always destined to be. I would like to **encourage** you to make a firm decision now, to BOLDLY continue your journey through life, to seek out your destiny, no matter what happens... promise yourself that you WILL KEEP MOVING **FORWARD**...even if you feel emotionally smashed into pieces, let this book give you the power you need....let the words fill you with passion and drive...use the different meditations to boost your spirit and always let your heart guide you towards the path you know to be right.... And draw **inspiration** from all I have written to continue boldly along that path even if you are in a dark place...and your mind is laced with negativity. Encourage yourself when nobody else will, I always encourage others to better themselves every single day. What have you done to encourage and drive yourself today?!?! I always strive to better myself physically, mentally, emotionally and spiritually. If you can do it, then you have a duty to and if you don't feel you can, be open to letting every sentence in this book **incite** you to move forwards. Cut through the barriers that are holding you back!

Please remember, if you have any concerns regarding your health and whether you can practice any of the deeper meditations that follow, and any of the physical exercises outlined or moving meditations, please consult your doctor first.

Energy Meditation – For creating a higher vibrational energy

I pray the words on this very page breathe **positivity directly** into every cell in your body! Having energy and drive in life is a worthy enough goal. If you know a goal is worthy of **pursuit**, for you, then **strive** to achieve it with 100% of your energy. And if your goal is for energy and the zest to live an amazing life, ALWAYS **step forward**, even if you feel you can't. Even if it is into the shadows of the unknown and uncertainty of confronting your fears head on. If the path you have envisioned feels right for you, TAKE IT! Do so with COMPLETE and UTTER conviction!!

I know some of you reading this will be my own students and you all have very different goals from each other. The **meditation**s are generic in nature and are designed to instil energy in all people who use them and give all people the tools that can be employed easily. My grandfather always said, all you need in life is determination!!!

Use **determination** to stay on the path, to spur you on and the meditation that follows supercharge your body with the energy to walk your chosen path. Everything in our universe, even our bodies, is composed of atoms. Our reality is measurable at the particle and energy level. While cells are the building blocks of life, atoms are the building blocks of everything else including cells! Atoms like the one drawn below, reside in all that exists and the subatomic particles within the atoms themselves, drawn as stars in the diagram below. Our physical world and the **energy** world are one in the same. Awareness of this simple fact will allow you to **engage** with the energetic world in a more profound and meaningful way.

1.To begin to attune yourself to energy, close your eyes and imagine your body is filled with little circular objects like the atom below.

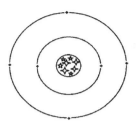

2. Imagine the atoms within your body are melting and fusing into the air all around you and you yourself connecting with the molecules in the air more intimately.

3. This visualisation and feeling of connectivity may manifest itself as a tingling sensation within all the dimensions of your body.

4. Feel connected to all the people, animals, plants and let your internal world fuse with all the dimensions of reality that exist. Allow any connection to become more powerful and aim to become more intimately linked to the consciousness that exists in both the physical and energy world.

3. Stay in this connected state, bask in it and enjoy the experience of oneness. This is what is called "Yoga" in India or true union.

Confidence with Xing Yi Quan, Old World Martial art stances for courage & exercises for empowerment

The stance I stand in the picture below is from the world of Xing Yi Quan, an aggressive and **powerful** internal martial art I was taught as part of my Kung Fu training. As a child, being overweight and of Asian origin, I looked different so I was bullied at primary school for several years. I was both physically assaulted and called hurtful names. The teachers in the school often heard and saw what was going on but turned a blind eye. It shook my confidence and I started resenting who I was and I felt I had no identity. I longed to train under masters of kung or Gung Fu and teachers of Karate like I had seen in films. I admired the way students, like me, who were subjected, persecuted, stood up for themselves and developed courage, strength and strong character. I became so fascinated by martial arts that I took up as many as I could and immersed myself in the training. I told nobody at school that I was learning. I did the same with Yoga, Tai Chi and meditation, because I wished to strengthen my mind and body. Furthermore, I wanted to take charge of my mind, emotions and re-kindle my spirit. The path of Xing Yi Quan leads to the creation of amazing levels of **power** and **courage**. If it could help a little boy whose spirit had been crushed, it could help anyone! And if I could drag myself to classes that developed me positively as a child, the least anyone can do is find the time to test and practice the exercises hereafter! Are you really too busy! Or are you pretending to be! Many people claim to be too busy because secretly their too afraid to make a change in case things get worse or their paralysed by the uncertainty of change. Xing Yi Quan is a little like Tai Ji Chaun but perhaps the opposite in many ways. It will fire you up! It will kick your spirit into action!! The stance below can change your body and mind in so many ways and like a Yoga asana it can help you harness phenomenal dimensions of power! It creates sharp crisp physical movement and greatly enhanced **responsiveness**. In case you were wondering, the bullies soon left me alone, perhaps because I stopped looking like a victim. And of course, I stood up for myself! My training helped me to become more **confident** and it showed in the way I held myself and behaved. Moreover, I was able to remain **calm** and **collected** through the whole of secondary school and talk with intelligence and self-assurance. I could confidently take myself away from hostility, without resorting to using the skills I trained in. For me...this was the true essence of martial art training! It was the life blood and spirit of a true martial artist. Martial arts is a discipline that advocates **control** and being able to walk away from trouble. With time we can learn how to build amazing rapport with even the most aggressive person, in order to interact in a beneficial and more meaningful way with all members of society. If you cannot understand aggression, fear and sadness in yourself, you will never be able to cope with them in others!!

Try the following exercise. It is based on Xing Yi Quan poses and meditation.

1. Stand or sit with one arm out stretched and the other at waist level as demonstrated in the photograph above.

2. Hold this position for as long as you can, **breathing slowly**, softly, using belly or diaphragmatic breath. Breathe in and out through the nose in a slow controlled manner.

3. Keep your eyes focused on a point in front of you. Your eyes must be **relaxed** but not dreamy....be focused but not on edge... be present and alert, in a state of readiness. And remain rooted in this energy for a while.

4. Remain still and focus on any physical sensations in your body and at the same time focus on the external experience. Feel the gentle **warmth** of the sun if you are outdoors and the muscle burn from the lactic acid building in your upper arms. Feel both outside and inside stimulation.

5. As you focus on the point in front of you and once your thoughts are a little more settled, in your mind say to yourself

three times "I command complete control over the energy that enters, leaves and resides in my body!" Say this as if you are talking to every single constituent carbon **atom** that comprises your body.

6. Say the following statement as a mantra three times "I fill my body with all the energy I require to **succeed** ALL aspects of life and create a positive impact in the lives of others"

7. Use the picture below to visualise your hero in life. Whoever it may be. Who is your hero? Perhaps a movie character, or maybe a friend or family member. Imagine this image is on a screen in your mind and envision the physical, mental, spiritual and emotional attributes of this individual are flowing into you from an image you have placed in the circle overleaf.

8. Imagine the lines represent pipes for flowing energy. Imagine the energy is flowing into an image of yourself, from your hero in life. Feel for the sensations you would expect to acquire form this individual. Imagine their energy is surging into your body and creating attributes in you that you most desire.

9. Breathe in and out slowly and imagine you are inhaling the energy that you need from your hero.

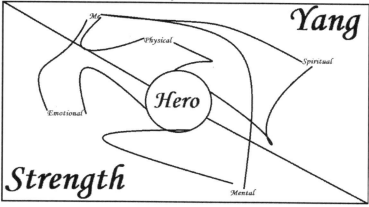

Remember, your subconscious mind cannot distinguish what is real and what is not. Saying anything over and over again, reinforces and makes it real in the mind. Just as the key words throughout this book create **positivity** within the readers mind subconsciously. **Xing Yi Quan** is not usually used as a still standing meditation as far as I am aware. I have added visualisation to this practice, to give you so much more courage and strength than still meditation alone! Old world martial artists, who are now few and far between, made students stand for long periods of time in a stance to develop their character as well as their **strength**. This is my own variation and traditional Xing Yi Quan is a little more dynamic, it is not usually used as a still meditation. However, I have found that adopting this mode of training was very effective at invoking powerful positive feelings and waves of **courage** and supreme discipline..... something many believe is impossible to acquire! Remember, meditation is not just for calming the mind, it can awaken you, sharpen your responsiveness and heighten your alertness.

How to deal with noise - meditation for concentration & managing stress

Let positivity always inflame and rouse you to continue along the path you know you are destined to take. Distractions will materialise the moment you set your intent to take a particular path in life. There are opposites to everything that we know to be real. Science tells us that to every force there is an equal and opposing force! Chinese philosophy told us this... centuries ago! And the YinYang nature of our world will invariably present itself to us **knowingly** or un**knowingly**. As a teenager, I was fortunate enough to have been introduced to meditation, Yoga and Tai Chi early on. I watched my mother practice Yoga and use acupressure for many different things, from pressure points for the common cold to general **wellbeing**. My mother also practiced and still does practice meditation and so too did other family members. I copied all that I could from them and created my own systems from what I had learnt, even before receiving professional training.

I loved to **meditate.** When I became a teenager, it helped to still my teenaged mind that was filled with a whole range of intense self-indulgent thoughts. I found it difficult to meditate not just for this reason but because I had one neighbour who moved in when I turned 13 and played loud music that would reverberate through the walls. Even late at night. Many times, it seemed like he would put it on at the exact time I wanted to meditate. I thought it was almost as though they knew and got a kick out of killing the peace! I would often think of people that claim not to be motivated enough to meditate. I was, but I had no space to do it!!!! I thought many times that perhaps it was a test from the divine! Perhaps the powers that be were watching how I might cope under this particular circumstance. I kept trying because I had nowhere else safe enough to go. The local park was full of muggers. I didn't want to experience awakening in hospital or in the next world! I did however make a firm decision to meditate and do WHATEVER it took to stay on that path I knew I was destined to take. I am glad I did so! Challenges still come my way to remove me from my path and I approach them in much the same way. **Meditating** with loud music around me actually helped my attention and spiritual **development** skyrocket. I was doing advanced level meditation early on. That is perhaps why I can deliver a class or session in the most challenging of environments to this day! I believe troublesome people and situations are sent into our lives to help us discipline ourselves in order to grow more strongly in a particular direction.

Do not let anyone or anything trouble your mind! Find a way to grow around them like a creeper or Japanese knot weed! If the trouble continues and you cannot get away from it what do you do? Here is the answer nobody seems to be willing to give the needy student.

You must use trouble to take you to the next level, let trouble treble the **focus** of your mind. Don't be anyone's....door mat.....! Let your motto be to ride waves of trouble and experience the joy of the surf. Use emergency to **emerge stronger** than ever before as you cut through into the dimensions of life others never dreamt you would!!! As my new neighbours played louder music, I continued to meditate and I even sat closer to the wall to feel more distracted. In doing so, I found that I was able to easily filter it out. Now, I always strive to create something good in all situations. And I love the saying "live life with **vigour** and joy." Always encourage a gutsy mindset and the **fortitude** to move toward what you want in life, regardless of what challenges are presented to you. If you do, the universe and God will help you gravitate towards your true divine purpose. Maybe this has hit home for one of my readers out there, so I repeat, "live with **vigour, joy** and **fortitude**. Use the image and meditation below to help to enhance your concentration and focus."

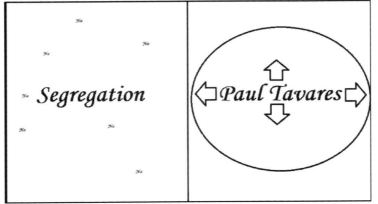

1. Read the following aloud 3 times to prepare and condition the mind.

- "I am open to using the noise around me to **developing** myself and in creating a highly focused mind."
- "I am **unphased** and stand strong and composed in noisy distracting places."
- "I meditate **easily** and I have the concentration power that is necessary to do so."
- "I am **passionate** about meditation and have the **enthusiasm** to turn everything others categorise as 'annoying' to my advantage."

2. Focus on the image above and try to imagine unionisation with all the noise around you. Try tuning into anything you observe in the way of sound. See yourself as two separate parts at first, then imagine the line or barrier separating the two energies, dissolving away slowly and steadily.

2. Now close your eyes and focus on your natural breathing rhythm, but focus more on how it sounds rather than how it feels......even if you can **barely** hear your breath in the midst of all the other noise.

3. Then shift your attention back on the music, noise or irritation.

4. Toggle between focusing on the music and your breath. 5. Repeat the process a few times.

6. Focus on any other noises.

7. Lastly, focus on your breathing alone with all the mental energy you can muster up to exercise the muscles of your brain!

Although there is unity within all the noise around you, this meditation will help you distinguish between the different sounds. It will ultimately help you to experience those sounds you wish to.

Calm, positivity & meditation for focus and changing the state of mind

Meditative disciplines are utilised to make people feel **happier**. They are primarily designed to calm troubled or busy minds by settling all the thought processes that make a mind overactive. It is well known that thoughts in the mind can alter the state of mind or how conscious you are in the world. Are you a conscious participant, or are you going with the flow? Flow is not necessarily a bad thing, but if it is someone else's and not the universe, you will never feel spiritually fulfilled my friend! A breakdown is perhaps the ultimate lapse in **consciousness** caused by negative emotions, next to states induced by disease and serious accidents. It is a complete loss of control and submission to entropy or disorder! Therefore, the intentional addition of positive thought to the mind can create the opposite effects and feelings. Positive **self-encouragement** is something we all hear about, but many do not apply the technique to their lives. Perhaps there is a part of us that wants to wallow in self-pity. If positive thoughts are added routinely, they can be experienced later, as positive emotions. Infusing the mind with positivity kick starts the bodies biochemistry to initiate the production of beneficial chemicals that are themselves, self-perpetuating. Always **infuse** your mind with the energy of positive thought whenever possible! Perhaps you should set aside a time of day when you practice positive self-encouragement. Look in the mirror right now and apologise to the vessel that is holding your spirit! What for!?!? For neglecting the need for recognition and for all the insults you have hurled at yourself throughout your life. If you were not able to think quickly enough and you have called yourself dumb, you are doing your mind a huge injustice. You are undermining your mind! If you say you hate your body, you are saying you hate the **temple** that has carried your spirit for so long without complaint. These aspects of yourself will not leave the world with you, so make peace with them first before you make peace with other vessels that have not carried the real essence of you!

Sometimes just a single thought can create very intense emotions in certain individuals, especially in those suffering from phobias. Conditions like arachnophobia, the fear of spiders, can create feelings so intense you break out in a sweat and become completely paralysed. I myself had a huge phobia of spiders as a child. If I knew there was one in my room, I couldn't sleep there. I eventually managed to overcome the fear. Though it was a very gradual process that involved facing my fears, sitting with spiders, **relaxing** around them and lowering my anxiety levels with time. The old saying "sticks and stones will hurt my bones but words will never hurt me" sounds like a statement that should be true, but in many cases, our need for approval from others around us, makes it a fallacy. In reality, only those who have attained a certain clarity within themselves can filter out all negativity from the external world. Meditation can provide a filtration system for the body that eventually unconsciously kicks in and creates **harmonisation**.

Thoughts can create so many different varieties of negative emotions....fear, worry, sadness included. The mind, body and emotion connection in a human being is something worth studying. Many cases of healing in one dimension and creating knock on effects in another have been well documented. We are all essentially the same in many ways, but some people might be more receptive to certain types of meditations than others. Emotions of certain mind diseases can literally cripple the physical body, to the extent that the person suffering can actually feel sensations of physical pain from a mind disorder. In the case of depression, the body can become filled with painful emotions that actually create physical pain in the body.

Whether the chemicals you unknowingly release into your body create a **positive** or negative effect, the resulting cocktail will cause some kind of physical, mental or spiritual stimulation and change. Both the activities of the mind and stimulation from the world we live in create our internal reality. Imagery, whether in the real world or played back images of the past, create feelings we experience in our bodies. Whatever the source, both image types can lead to emotional pain in the form of stress, unease or anxiety. So, conscious actions toward the attainment of positive goals, in the form of thoughts or physical experiences in the world, have the "**power**" to manifest and propagate in many ways that are beneficial.

Try the following meditation for changing your state of mind. Use the diagram below as a meditation aid.

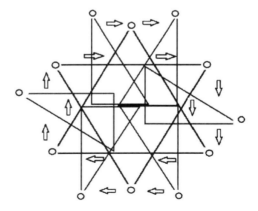

1. Keep your eyes open and begin by sitting or lying and concentrate on remaining as still as possible. No need to focus on

your breathing and no need to even watch your thoughts. Just keep your body still.

2. Breathe in for a count of 10, hold for 5 and breathe out for 15. Do this for around 10 cycles. Still keeping your eyes open and remaining as still as possible.

3. Focus on your natural breathing pattern.

4. Look directly at the middle of the above and see the outer rim with your prereferral vision. It is a mandala, or shape that can be used to create deep meditative states of mind. Focus on the centre of the star shaped mandala and at the same time repeat a meaningful word or saying to yourself, like a mantra.

3. Start to focus on each of the small circles at each point around the rim of the shape, one by one for 9 seconds. Count to 9 in your mind then move to the next in the direction of the arrows.

4. Repeat stage 3 until you have completed 6 revolutions in total. If your attention drifts, just refocus yourself by looking at the middle of the star once more. In particular, look at the dark line between the large and small triangle if your attention drifts. Then continue focusing on the circles moving from one to the next, until you have finished 6 whole revolutions.

5. Your eyes will feel tired, close them, but concentrate on your breathing for another minute or so.

Relaxation programs, balance and YinYang

Many generic relaxation programs, classes, sessions and guided meditations will talk you through a process in which you envision walking on a beach, through a garden, by a stream or by a lake. This creates a very calming and relaxing effect for the meditator, as places filled with nature create feelings of inner peace and **tranquillity**.

Try this very simple meditation.

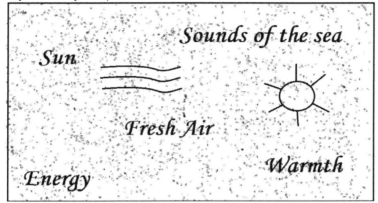

Look at the picture above for a while and use it to prompt the meditation process that follows.
1. Attentively observe your breath for a couple of minutes.
2. Imagine a beach you have visited in the past and imagine lying on it, in the early morning sun.
3. Imagine the rays of the sun are healing and nurturing. Let them infuse you with energy.
4. Hear the gentle sound of the waves, seagulls and imagine each inbreath of revitalising restorative sea air.
5. In your mind, imagine relaxing in this lovely place for as long as you wish.

Having studied behavioural psychology, I have been able to identify real examples of people who create feelings of **calm** and

relaxation associations with places they feel happy in. And in particular when they are in touch with nature. Events can be enriched with positive associations or tarnished with negative ones. These associations develop because we create emotions in tandem with the events we experience in life. When similar events are experienced again, they illicit a particular type of feeling inside, as a result of this conditioning. And the more you reinforce the memory with intense feelings, the more powerful the sensation and emotional link to the same feelings. Serious life experiences like living through a war or a natural disaster and seeing people die can have a profound impact on an individual's persona and their mode of behaviour. Their whole personality can change because personality is linked strongly to feeling.

I want to show you how to create COMPLETE **control** over your **mind**. Few have complete mastery over the mind, because we believe there is not enough time to nurture this aspect of our development. There are some events that can shake the mind **substantially**. But, if you take steps toward re-stabilising the mind, I honestly believe anyone can get to a level that is far better than where we are at the moment. This level of governance over yourself can be achieved by fusing two meditation types together. That is, the classic inert/passive style of control in regular meditation and couple it with the super authoritative energy of power meditation! My power meditation is a modality that directly whips the mind into shape. What does it involve? Having read so far into this book you are already practicing it, if you tried any of the meditations up to this point.

I am not saying anyone can achieve perfection and I'm not claiming to be perfect, but I am certainly able to cope far better than a regular person. And that is why many have asked me to teach them ways to cope more effectively with the challenge's life presents to them. Instead of soul searching or searching for yourself gently, this book will teach you how to **dynamically** root out the problems tormenting you! I want to show you how to command and redirect your thoughts for your better evolution as a holistic being and use them to **supercharge** you into taking a more conscious active role in this world.

It is a common belief that relaxation and strength are opposites and cannot function coupled together. Relaxation can be a strength and strength can create relaxation. But it is thought by many that one opposes the other. I am sure that many ancient cultures would disagree with this notion. Ancient Chinese culture describes and understands the interplay of opposites at the deepest level. The so-called opposing energies can **coexist** in harmony, as does everything at this point in time in our reality. And this is the philosophy and way of YinYang or Tai Chi. The symbol below is a representation of YinYang. YinYang can be drawn either way, i.e. one that rotates clockwise or counter clockwise. I prefer counter clockwise because then energy behind it seems to fit with my own at this point in time. I like to mimic nature and the natural flow of energy through it. Hurricanes move counter clockwise in the Northern Hemisphere and clockwise in the Southern Hemisphere. So as to align with nature and pull more energy into my body, I tend to meditate on YinYang in a counter clockwise direction. I was also told by my teachers that counter clockwise is the true direction of flow and the original way to draw and represent YinYang.

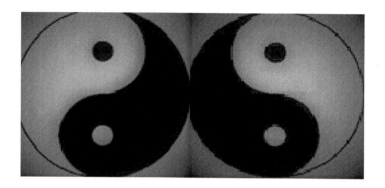

Look deeply into one of the symbols above for a while. And use this time to contemplate how everything in the universe exists. Everything in the physical world exists in a state of **dynamic** movement. There is also an opposite to everything. Take a few minutes to appreciate this fact and the generic nature of the symbol YinYang. Now think of internal opposites.... emotions.... thoughts.....sensations and beliefs. In this way, you can learn to explore the inner depths of yourself and create the true inner self you desire.

I asked many of my teachers the question where YinYang came from? Many did not have a definitive answer. So, I would answer "it is unclear how the symbol YinYang was born, although there are many theories".

I believe that all symbols have a certain **energy** that metaphorically represents something different to each person. Even words hold power and the way they are read can give them even more power. Everyone has their own spin on how to interpret any and all things in life. Our interpretations create our own individual plight in life and the way view the world. For me, balance is having invigorating and relaxing energies. You can position yourself in a place better able to deal with life if you have both energies at your disposal as and when you want. If you aim to minimalize what life gives you in excess, you are going against the natural flow of life. Try and learn from what you are given so as to exist at a level that is higher than one which is mediocratic. Being able to call forth the energy of either **strength** or **relaxation** at will is a power unto itself.

There are so many distorted views and ideas relating to many symbols and their meanings. You can attach any meaning to any arbitrary symbol, depending on what your view of the symbol and the culture it came from. I **love** Chinese culture and I love the many lovely interpretations I have heard from Chinese masters and friends relating to this symbol. The emblem below is slightly different from YinYang, one might even call it YangYin. The subtle difference is noticeable and perhaps nice to sit and think about as a contemplative meditation. Perhaps think of a world where strength is weakness in the literal sense and weakness is strength. Whatever storms we go through in life, there is usually a turning point where yin changes to yang and vice versa, that is, the storm subsides.

When I look at YinYang, I think very deeply. I often think that extra-terrestrials viewing the planet see it as a big blood bath tempered with some love! How? When we move from A to B, we kill thousands of plants, insects and microscopic lifeforms. We stamp unknowingly upon them, without the intent to hurt them. We care for certain animals like dogs and cats. But we chase rats away and set traps for them. Perhaps we do so for reasons that are seemingly good to us, but, not if we truly valued all life and look at the world from the mouse or rats' point of view! Destructive and constructive energies must coexist in our convoluted world. YinYang teaches us to embrace the storms of life and make living **amazing**.

YinYang reminds us that meditation can both **rejuvenate** and **empower** people. Or perhaps do both simultaneously. A good understanding of this interplay of opposites is what is necessary to apply the Tai Chi philosophy perfectly to your life.

Life as a meditator

Meditation and self-development are often lonely activities. Meditating is an exploratory task for the individual who will slowly gain a better understanding of their own bodily functions. Gradually, with dedication and discipline you will master the ability to self-create feelings of happiness, joy and peace with little or no effort at all.

If you manage to reach this stage, you will be able to tread many paths happily and achieve many greater things. You will have achieved a highly respectable level in your spiritual journey and quest for fulfilment. It is well worth investing **devoted** time and effort in yourself this way. The world has no place for traits that are undesirable or those that do not make a useful **contribution** to it. Always think holistically and at the macroscopic level. Ask yourself the question, is this beneficial for both myself and all others? If your answer is yes then you will ultimately be in a good energetic alignment with the natural flow of the universe, you will empower others positively through your actions, thereby making a very useful contribution indeed. Never waste time in self-pity or feeble blame games. Use all negative emotions you experience as signs that you ought to drive yourself in a different way, perhaps harder or not so much. Use negativity to understand at a deeper level, what you truly need. Perhaps you will get to the stage where you can tune into subtle pain before it presents itself as a serious pain in the physical body. Or maybe you can address feelings of sadness early on before they cascade into the overwhelming feelings **experienced** in depression.

Soldiers understand the irrelevance of feelings that are troublesome, especially when you have to survive a war. But they also recognise that every feeling is important and did not remain in the current pool of evolution for nothing. All feelings that are created by chemical signals require conscious or unconscious reaction. If the emotions get too intense, they control us and cause us to behave in a particular way. **Be a soldier for life,** be in command and always consider the positive benefit of all human beings. Whatever your **goals** may be, physically, mentally, emotionally, spiritually, if you have something you really want in life; the meditations throughout this book will give you the energy to get it. Know that you are a work of art in progress. You will create the mindset of a champion, of a go-getter, regardless of how you are feeling, you will be able to press forward.

Triangles are very powerful objects. In nature fire and the destruction, it brings, is feared by ALL sentient beings. Something we all have in common with other beings that are instructed by the base sequences within DNA. Fire needs three things to sustain itself.... a fuel, oxygen from the air and heat. If the three components of fire sat in the corners of a triangle, it is said that taking one component away will cause the triangle to collapse and the fire to die. Yet together, the components create a formidable force that is near unstoppable.

Try the following meditation and use the triangle below to assist you:
1. Think of three people you look up to and imagine their names or **essence** is sitting at the corner of the triangle. Perhaps, you could even write them in the book if it belongs to you. Maybe

these individuals are people who have achieved what you want to achieve. Perhaps they have reached a level you strive to attain.

2. Think of the traits they each possess.

3. Close your eyes. Imagine you are each person in turn.

4. Imagine what it would be like to possess each of the traits in turn. What does the **energy** of each trait feel like? Try and imagine what it feels like to hold all the traits of your champions in life.

5. Once you have done this for several traits each hero has, say the following affirmation 10 times "I have developed the same traits of my heroes and role models"

6. Now imagine the positive energies you want from each person sitting at the corners of the triangle. Focus on your breathing for a minute and with each inbreath imagine pulling in the energies of the traits you wish to embody. Perhaps you can assign a colour to each trait or group of traits.

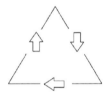

Each time you decide to meditate, look forward to the process. Any session is going to be beneficial. Remember, nobody can force you to **like** something unless you are open to enjoying it.

<u>Be bold, be a warrior and punch your way to positivity!</u>
Listed within the text below are a series of paragraphs that offer
much **positive insight** and **inspiration**.....as well as more
powerful mind, body, emotion and spirit exercises that will help
YOU establish COMPLETE **dominion** you're your emotional state.

If you believe you are predestined to achieve something
incredible in this life, then why not give life your best attempt.
Start to live your life and don't let others live it for you! I talk to
people from all walks of life. Some are undermining, but I realise
that sometimes people are going through things that are worse
than I can possibly imagine. Or they are just having a bad day.
And it is my life mission to help people control and steer
themselves through life in a calm and fulfilled manner. If you have
to work on yourself, so that you are better able to deal with the
world and others, then do it. You must. But if you are already in a
state to create great things then you need to stop working
internally so much, get out of yourself and do something in the
real world!! There is only so much meditating you can do.

Live with complete connection with as much as you can in this
world and push ahead. Place one foot in front of the other as you
simultaneously address the problems and barriers in your path.
Always remember you are the driver of the vehicle; others are
back seat drivers. Be **bold** and **decisive!** Stand strong as I am in
the picture below. I remember a speech from one of my favourite
WWE wrestlers, Mr Warrior. One sentence stuck out for me. He
said, "do you dare to step into the darkness of the unknown".
Two weeks before he died, I had been corresponding with him.
The last message he sent me was via e-mail and it read, "Paul,
you know what you must do". I think we all know what we need
to do in life, but few of us do. You know what you need to do to
achieve your goals! So, go do it!

> *You know what you must do!*

Never ever let anyone annoy, irritate or frustrate you. Be strong enough to either ignore those that oppose you and say no to injustice. I know it is not easy. Everyone struggles with their demons. Not so much in the metaphysical sense unless you are being **spiritually** tested, more as physical manifestations of yin or darkness. I think that even if you are not religious, you can take a lot from the teachings of Jesus. Especially when he says get behind me Satan, to those people he trusted when they show their darker sinister nature.

Let meditation settle your **mind** and my "power meditations" condition you with the strength of assertiveness.
Remember that the form you inhabit is composed of a mind, body, **emotions** and a spirit. And subdivisions of each. Even when you are exasperated, with tears in your eyes say to yourself "I can do this, I **FIRE UP** my spirit and I WILL get through this because I will do what it takes and I have the energy". Shout this at the top of your voice if you can!! Perhaps into the imaginary eyes of those who wish to crush your spirit. But do it from a space of love. You should respect others, but you should not be a door mat. Your spiritual energy will get you through even the darkest of times, if you keep it fuelled with meditation, affirmations, mantras and prayer if you are religiously inclined. Make sure your spiritual cup is full and those who mock you will be the ones who suffer.

Karate – Empty Hand meditation

Fire up your mind daily in any way you can, even if you feel broken, bashed up and cracked into pieces. Find your own unique way to leave a trail of sparks behind you on your road to victory. Attempt with all your **energy,** to break through dark clouds, address the feelings of being broken and rise again. Become whole once more and MAKE SURE you enhance the **enormity** of what you can do in this world! Sometimes picking up the pieces just does not work and you need to use a different strategy.

Try the following Karate style exercise for courage:

1.Make fists with your hands.

2. Imagine a punch bag hanging in front of you.

3. **Punch** towards it starting slowly then increasing your speed.

4. Make sure not to lock your arms at the elbow completely to prevent damage to your joints.

5. Increase the energy behind the punch.

6. Imagine you are punching through wood with ease.

7. Imagine punching a hole through metal, concrete and diamond.

If you think this meditation is silly, or not worth trying you are not operating at the level of a champion. A champion is someone who lives life and is not used by it.

I want you to have COMPLETE **authority** over all dimensions of yourself! Keep reading on and learn to shift your mindset at will. Learn to rule your mindset easily and effortlessly!

Discipline your mind because nobody else will!

Sometimes, if the gentle approach is not working, you need to CLOUT your mind into shape. You need to force discipline upon it! Based on my observations through instructing, helping and teaching groups of people achieve their potential, I can CONFIDENTLY say that those who employ the methods I have outlined above can EXPECT to achieve **tremendous positive benefits** in 99.999% of cases.

But there are many more techniques hereafter. Regular meditation in the way I describe throughout this book will cause you to start to replicate and command **positive thoughts** into your mind unconsciously. You will be able to influence and rule your emotions, thoughts and behaviours and allow them to manifest uncontrollably like a virus. Positive thoughts will become self-perpetual. Let this book **positively infect** all aspect of your life in which you feel **power**less in. Viruses whether they infect computers or living beings replicate and spread at phenomenal speeds. Let this book have the same effect in your life but take a positive route.

You know, I cannot guarantee you an easy ride through life. Who can? I do not think any earthbound red-blooded human being can make such a pledge, yet. However, I can promise you will **triumph** in one way. You will learn how to make problems sit in the background while you harness the energy to move in the foreground and I will also teach you to raise your spirits and boost your motivation.

I have given you tools that enrich you with the energy of **confidence** to achieve your goals with a level of thirst and **passion** you have never felt in yourself before! You will start to learn to pull your problems inside out with fury!!! You will start to connect with the universe and all of God's creation to craft inside yourself explosive energies of **desire**, **determination** and **discipline**. Think of these three "d's" as the corners of a triangle and every so often, check in on yourself and make sure you do all you can to create the three energies within you. Perhaps carry the image of the triangle below in your mind's eye. Make sure your focus is on it and the energy of the three words of power. On awakening keep this image clearly in your mind and if you do perhaps you will experience true "**awakening**" in the way of enlightenment or nirvana.

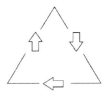

Soon, if you have not started already, you WILL begin to address ANY and ALL problems in a more detached and less reactive manner. You will be gently responsive, more methodical and with heightened alertness. Maybe you already feel you have a stronger level of control over your life having meditated in the ways I have taught you, and maybe you already have achieved many goals. If that is the case, go and take a holiday and think of your next conquest....!!

Conscious positive action & Power Affirmations

Say the following affirmation to yourself three times, right now: **"I storm through life with confidence as I am in complete alignment with the plan of God and I feel divinely guided by the natural flow that directs all that exists. Therefore, I**

accomplish ALL my aspirations with the support of God and intelligent effort!" If you are not into religion you can modify the statement accordingly perhaps adding universe or the powers that be. I believe in higher powers and I have had plenty of great experiences with Jesus Christ, but I am no better than any other human being and we are all on a unique individual journey. Let's not make the journey any more difficult for anyone else than it already is.

Being reactive is more animalistic than human. Human beings are evolutionary diamonds. Being the only animals in the world to have colonised space, created fire at will and harnessed the energy of the world in unique and innovative ways. Only animals respond in a reactive un**thoughtful** manner and are considered more primitive the more reactive they are. Science considers the reptile brain to be older than that of their mammalian counterparts and perhaps more primitive. Reptiles attack without a thought in their mind, so react rather than think and respond. If you touch a crocodile while it is basking in the sun, it will snap you up without question. Even if you just wanted to give it a stroke!

Mammals are considered more complex and undergo a more complex thought processes before they decide what to do, so as human beings and we should, as higher beings, be even more responsive and controlled. Surely, we, as the most **powerful** beings on this planet, can learn to respond rather than be controlled like puppets by all that happens around us. Can't we? The more controlled we are the less intelligent we are in terms of emotional control. Too much control and lack of expression makes us robotic and more like walking computers. So, it is better to strike a balance and find a way to interact that sits between the two extremes. Getting annoyed if someone cuts in front of you while driving on the road shows you are yourself out of control. You should be cross with yourself and use that rage to fuel your own personal development. Perhaps you are in a better state than someone else, but you can still establish a better level of **restraint** followed by **conscious positive action**. Let us finish this section with one final affirmation you can use to keep responsive rather than reactive. **"I think before I act and I respond intelligently, where possible, to situations presented to me by the external world."**

Redevelop yourself Using Ancient Powerful Systems – Kalari & Snake style Kung fu

If you have lost your self-esteem, physical strength or motivation, I will help you recover it. I want you to vow to reclaim territory you have lost in any area of your life. Wherever that territory may reside, I want you to do all you can to reclaim it once more.

Let the completion of this very paragraph be a declaration and a **COMPLETE** turning point in your life. Resolve to change your mind set NOW! I want you to make a pledge to yourself to regain what you have lost. Make a commitment. **Commit** to **positive transformation** today and to becoming an amazing megastar of your life!!

Modify any areas of yourself that you dislike in your life in any way you can and adjust yourself to become a person others never imagined you would be! Continue to use this book and the meditation techniques religiously and adjust the time when you meditate to fit in with your schedule. If all hell is breaking lose, meditate in the eye of the storm, with tears in your own eyes and even the divine will salute you. As you have probably guessed, I am here to expound the belief that meditation is not just for relaxation and searching for yourself. **Meditation** can help you take huge leaps forward towards a goal, break barriers and make an amazing impact in the world.

Kalaripayattu (Kalari) is an ancient martial art from India. I was pleased to hear of an Indian lineage in the martial art world. Kalari was the first martial art to have ever been created and was taken to China by a master called Bodhidharma. Bodhidharma is not acknowledged near enough as he should be, I believe he needs a far bigger place in the martial art world. There are martial art communities who have never even heard of him! To not honour the founder of martial arts is a huge injustice.

India is known for so many wonderful people and disciplines including Yoga. But many have not even heard of Bodhidharma, nor have they heard of **Kalari**. Kalari is yet another wonderful discipline India has to offer the world. And it is the foundation through which all the other martial arts originated. As someone who knows the forms of the ancient world as well as a modern version of Kalari along with applications, I would be overjoyed to bring this discipline to people everywhere.

When I train in Kalari, I use old world training coupled with meditation. Masters and instructors of the past in many parts of the world would watch animals and mimic the way in which they fight. I see Kalari as an empty hand and meditative discipline as well as a combative art with formidable weaponry. Martial artists of the old world, including practitioners of Kalari, would embody the **energy** of a particular animal by mimicking its movements. I learnt snake style Kung Fu from a Chinese teacher who owned a restaurant close to where I lived in Clapham Junction as a child.

She taught me not just movements but how to use the positive aspects and essence of the snake itself. When I think of snake style energy, I think of the CONSTANT intelligence and concentration it has. Kung Fu took the Kalari animal styles to another level and the **evolution** of martial arts is a beautiful subject of study. Snakes, just as other animals have their own unique speciality and energy. In Kalari there are 9 animals I know of, on which fighting techniques are based. We will not discuss the martial applications further in this book as the objective is meditation, however, you can use meditation to place your mind in the best possible state for combat and competition fighting.

Try the following meditation – It allows a devotee to invoke and embody the energy of animals used in Kalari forms:

1.Look at the diagram below depicting the 9 animals of Kalari.
2.Spend a minute or so looking and meditating on each word or animal moving clockwise round the ellipse.
3.Think of the **energy** associated with each animal in turn and try to **conjure** it up using your imagination. Perhaps you can imagine what it would feel like to be fearless before an interview or public speaking....
4.Imagine **absorbing** the energy deep into yourself, just use your imagination. If you have trouble imagining this or visualising the animal itself, perhaps you can watch some wildlife documentaries first, this will help you with the envisioning process.

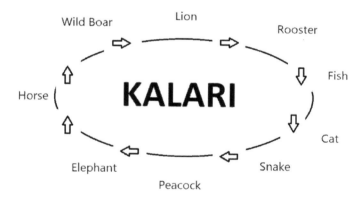

Meditation this way can make you sharper and bind you with **electrifying positive energy**. Problems will be something you are now equipped to solve routinely. The meditation above is like a tool kit with devices that solve an entire range of problems.

Each animal has energies and traits you can call upon to give you a particular energy to solve a particular problem.

You will soon become your own greatest, unsurpassed guru. Let suffering NEVER numb your pre-eminent **drive** and **determination**. Keep using the meditation above whenever you feel low on any particular energy. I have created this modern meditation based on the oldest martial art to honour the discipline and its founder, master Bodhidharma. Remember, we all evolved from an animal like state and we can activate the primitive yet powerful **energy** within any of our genes associated with this state through meditation! We can create a higher vibrational state by using "lower level" energy traits! Those who criticise energy work will tell you otherwise, but remember, **science** does not have all the answers. And, it is science that tells us everything is made of energy......and in the modern world numerous religious leaders now advocate the use of meditation for many mind disorders. As the old saying goes, I would always opt for meditation as a supplement for medication, if I had the option.

Super powerful drive & "Junk DNA" energy meditation

Commit to **harness** the energy of discipline and let the energy of outstanding drive latch onto your psyche. **Unstoppable determination** can **dispel** procrastination, suffering and any and all mind body emotion and spirit problems if the will is to get better. Others will recognise a change in you and you yourself will watch the world **stand** still as you **shine** like a **star**. There are many stars in the sky, blue, white, orange and red. They all sparkle white from a distance, lets compete with the heavens collectively, whatever colour we are. Let us fill this world with **super stars** and become a collective sparkling sphere, metaphorically, shining with positivity, brighter than any part of God's universe.

Persist, reclaim what you have lost and draw positivity into yourself even if you have to wrench it in! I want you to feel **encouraged** if you feel discouraged. Use the techniques daily and strive to create daily, a state of **euphoria**. I cannot stress the importance of learning what really works or perhaps what works for you. Some people believe they have got to the highest level and cannot go any further. Then they stop growing and evolving. They believe their minds are saturated with all the information they can assimilate. Get to the level you believe you were destined to, but keep exercising the muscles of your mind, moving towards a higher level and refocus yourself on something else. What is the next goal? Strive to achieve it! Not for your own happiness but for your evolution and the benefit of all mankind.

Try the following exercise. All living things are controlled by genes clustered along a DNA double helix. This molecule sits in the nucleus of all the cells within our body:
1.Study the picture below, preferably first thing in the morning.

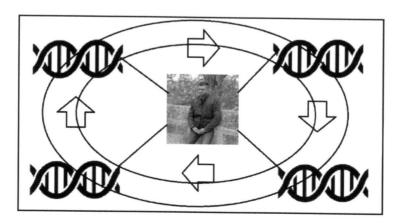

2. Sit comfortably and imagine the many strands of **DNA** inside your body.

3. Imagine the sections of the strands that **create positive** states of mind. Imagine they are lighting up and instructing the body to create sensations of happiness and delight. You don't need to know exactly where scientifically, just use your mind and **imagination**. Your body will recognise the intent and your intuition will douse for and activate the correct area within you.

4. Imagine this is a very real experience. Use the image above to focus your mind on what DNA looks like and to visualise this gene activation process. Remember the more you practice the better you will become. Any doubts in your mind should be placed aside.

5. If you have a low immune system, perhaps you can imagine the genes for creating immune cells from your bone marrow coming on and attacking any and all viruses and/or non-beneficial bacteria that invade the body. A better way, although not so scientific, would be to imagine activating a gene that sends the energy of evolution, cooperation and love to any and all entities, viruses included!

6. Now, bask in the feelings of positivity.

7. Start your day.

Discipline and planning for goals/cutting out damaging behaviour.

A settled mind may be the worst and most damaging state of mind for some, because **settling** the mind makes it stagnate. Most people conform to the idea of holidaying until the sun, sea, fun and games dull your mind to the level that you can't even remember what day it is!

Always work the mind in the most powerful way you can! Even on holiday! Of course, you need to have fun, but **discipline** is something you should never ever forsake!! It is the key to massive success, even when it comes to taking an amazing holiday. Why not take the energy of discipline with you and holiday in style!! Maybe being unsettled, eager, thrilled and wound up can be a positive experience for many. That is if you are still experiencing **happiness** in this state! Some people truly thrive in a pressure filled environment. They just love it!

Perhaps there may be one particular type of problem or challenge that keeps presenting itself to you over and over again. Have the discipline to work on developing skills you do not have yet or techniques to curtail a problem or particular destructive behaviour. Regardless of how many times that issue has crushed you in the past. Persistence is the key to overcoming any obstacle and creating **happiness** while experiencing this event in ANY WAY YOU CAN.

Nothing is without an opposite or weakness. You now have at your disposal, a range of highly effective tools within this book that you can **deploy** to manage, **circumvent** and eventually **eradicate** the feelings of being **power**less from in life!! No matter who you are or what your age, I want you to at least try. Perhaps you will become an inspiration to everyone around you. You never know who you will inspire through your own behaviour. I believe the world opens many more doors of opportunity to givers. Perhaps acting with the right discipline may inspire a child, a sibling or maybe even your own child.

I have ALWAYS functioned like an explorer in life. That is why I initially chose to study science, **genetics** and biochemistry at degree level. And as a scientist, I have learnt to search and **discover** reasons why everything **functions** in a particular way and the very reason why we exist.......i.e. what the process of life actually is? Questions like...why are we here? Do we have purpose? What is this process we call life all about? Questions like this have always fascinated me. Now, I look for answers to such questions all the time, but I don't get too caught up in thought processes and the ways of the world, that is, I also live my life to the fullest being fully focused and engaged in all that I do, regardless of how "I feel". And when I do this, soon enough, I feel **great** or I look back on what I have done and feel grateful that I did not stop and wallow in my own self-pity.

As a person who embodies and enjoys open-mindedness and exploring the alternate ways of reasoning ....I have come to believe more strongly in a higher power, **God**, universal energy or whatever you call that which created everything, through all the experiences I have had. I may discuss these experiences in detail in another book. I have always been religious and was born and raised a Catholic.

I still attend church. I love the Catholic faith. I do like many religions too and have the deepest respect for all understandings of life and belief systems that **perpetuate** and **preach** love. I also enjoy exploring my **spirituality** and have had amazing experiences on my own path. I think many reading this book can identify with me. I have observed that many people often lapse in **faith** and turn away from anything remotely **spiritual** when something goes seriously wrong in their life. Perhaps some believe that certain negative forces are deliberately trying to break them for some purpose that is unbeknown to us. I believe this may sometimes happen.... But I would **strongly** DISAGREE that our personal understanding at this point in time is complete.... Things are not ideal according to our understanding as human beings, but perhaps they are the way they need to be according to the divine and the powers that be. Perhaps our notion of what is positive is far from the truth or perhaps it was our decision to experience and inhabit a world tainted with negativity, else we would never know what positive was. Always consider what thoughts you **add** into your mind...because some thought processes can become quite damaging for anyone to hold within. Perhaps the tree of life shed light on a world where negativity became a reality and so began the cycles of YinYang and samsara.

Positivity connectivity and alignment

Negative **attention**, creates brainwaves (energy) of a particular type that gets deliberated in all planes within us that make us human...i.e. the mind...body...emotion and spirit become **influenced** by all energies. The energy of despair, dejection and hopelessness can manifest itself in a range of mind related and physical disorders. Avoid this type of slump at all costs. If you cannot, and the environment around you is such that you are subjected to negative energies routinely, then you need to meditate more than everyone else. Be disciplined and take massive action to stop the negative processes from happening "to you" in any way you can, even if they are happening "around you". I believe that the higher powers and God encourage a plight or journey that ultimately **coax** us into the creation of self-sustained positivity and pleasure.... perhaps to avoid any type of regression. Maybe this is Gods way of expanding us through making us more independent as we would our own child. We can create our own pleasure even in the midst of unhappiness. I have seen many people do this even under very difficult circumstances. Whatever our life path, we can always strive to create the energy of **discipline,** so we grow the way we want to. When discipline is used to create positive routines, you are on the road to victory. You can always rescue yourself from a downward spiral, provided you truly want to.

I pray and encourage you to strive to pass your unique tests in life and ultimately the spiritual examination. If your life is full of darkness at present. Take the challenge. Live your life to the fullest, move towards your goals, come what may, find light in darkness and a way to **amplify** that light. How do you find the light? If you are in a very dark place you need to keep searching for the right formula. Find the right meditation and techniques just as a doctor will search for the right antibiotic to overcome a bacterial infection of some kind. That is what a true sentient and evolving being requires. Become a beacon of **positive vibrant energy** for yourself and an example for others. If you had one day left, what would you do with that day? This is a great question to ask yourself in order to weed out frivolous tasks form your life. Shine the light of positivity towards your goals. Consciously leave a trail of energetic specs along the path you take and know to be right, so that others less motivated or less fortunate can follow that same path. I know these statements sound poetic and perhaps intangible, but they work if you are willing to put in the time and effort.

I believe life is an attempt by the divine powers that be to understand how we human beings and our collective **consciousness** can function within different environments and situations? Perhaps it is an attempt to **analyse** the way we respond to all that is presented to us and how far we can evolve. Rather like a **science** experiment. It is my hope that you will find meaning and courage in even the most adverse of events and consequently find the strength to participate in this experiment positively and support others who cannot cope. It is better to try and fail than sit on the fence and do nothing.

I have a friend who teaches children in India who live on the street how to create works of art from litter. The children make toys and **amazing** structures from anything and everything they find. They create beautiful structures from plastic bottles, empty wrappers etc and go on to sell it for a wage. I hope the techniques outlined in this text will provide you the tools to make massive changes in your life regardless of whether your situation seems truly rubbish. I hope you can create better structure in your life just as the street children in India created **amazing** works of art with the little, they have.

Never carry hate in your heart. Defiant or obstructive energy that opposes the natural flow created by **God** in the universe, will only diminish once you make a decision to enter a state of alignment with that energy and your values. I love the biblical Psalm 91, "Trust in God and you will trample down even fierce lions and poisonous snakes" If you establish any resistance to the natural flow.... You would, in a roundabout way demonstrate contempt for creation itself and the creative **force** behind it if you go against the natural flow. You would put yourself out of alignment with the energy that created everything and **intelligence** of our creator.... So, the energy of hindrance in some way is bound to follow you around. If you do not trust in God as Psalm 91 outlines quite nicely for us.

Try practicing the following meditation:
(1) Study the picture portraying our solar system below.

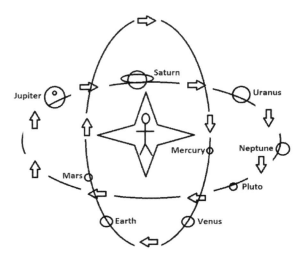

(2) Sit or lie down in a quiet place.
(3) Imagine rings or belts of **energy** circling round your body. Like conveyer belts. Imagine they are orbiting from your head to your tail bone, around your hips and around your joints. In ancient Chinese medicine the joints are said to sit inside rings of **energy**.
(4) Imagine you are right in the middle of our solar system, in the centre of the sun, basking in the energy of the sun. Sit there and experience the powerful white light of this star that keeps our planet alive.
(5) Imagine the same loops of energy circling round your body and the luminous glowing Sun that surrounds you. Feel like you are connecting with the physical planets around you as they make their orbit and extend your connectivity to the universe.

(6) Feel completely connected with everything and in your mind say to yourself "I am connected to the natural energy flow of the universe and I align all that I do subconsciously with this positive flow." "Opportunities come to me routinely and I act on intuition to take those that align with my highest purpose".

Inspiration through focus

Loving the **present** will present you with more potential opportunities you can ever imagine. But what do we really mean by loving the present? The present is constantly in a state of evolution. How can we know at what exact time we are in the present and when it has turned into the past?

When masters talk about the here and now, they mean integration and connection with everything simultaneously. It is to use all your 5 senses and experience as much as you can. Martial artists and soldiers understand this feeling because you need to be fully present when you are fighting an opponent. I am talking about old style martial arts, when there were less health and safety regulations. When I started martial arts, sparring was done with bare knuckles and if you were hit you would feel it!! You would be fully integrated with yourself and connect with anything useful that could help you survive! I tried an amazing new Russian martial art recently for a year called Cystema that advocates bare knuckle training in a controlled manner. Fight the present and create a battle you cannot win. Fight to be present and you will create a life you need not battle to live.

Genuinely love the moment and be open to intuitive and perhaps divine guidance in the direction that is suitable for you as an evolving **spiritual** being. Be open and receptive and have the mental conviction to always affirm what you want and repel that which is not suitable for you. Affirm what you want aloud, so your subconscious mind can hear the message clearly. Just before you sleep you can try saying the following in your mind **"I am open to divine guidance I will be present enough to notice messages sent from my guides for my growth and development as a spiritual being. I will thereafter intuitively respond to what is correct by the standards of God and all that is righteous"**

Of course, I myself am on my own personal journey and I am constantly applying and refining the techniques I teach. And I ALWAYS remember that life may not begin or end like a perfect movie made by Hollywood or Bollywood directors, but if you interact fully with the present and strive to do the best you can...... I am certain your life movie will become a best seller in the watchful eyes of the divine.....

Each paragraph hereafter will be like a SUPERCHARGED dose of positivity and inspiration for you. Let the key words work subconsciously at THE DEEPEST level to **instil positivity** in you.

SPOON FEED your mind constantly to push yourself onto the path of victory! Don't ever allow anyone to feed you lies that take you away from your goals. School yourself in any way that will help. Ignore anything and all things that misdirect you. **Maximise** your intake of positive energy daily by feeding yourself what information from books and videos to encourage yourself. Dismount the negative treadmills of **life** and move onto the road to **liberation** to an illuminated process of life. My father passed away a few years ago and as a child he had always wanted me to do what makes me **happy** and content. And he always wanted me to stand up for what is **correct**, **ethical** and for my rights as a human being.

I love to extend my joy to others. When you are in a highly positive frame of mind, you can literally infuse others with feelings of joy and contentment...that is, let the same energy rub off on others. Positivity and negativity are as infectious as a yawn or disease! **Emotional rapport** is just as powerful as physical rapport. Many times, my students and clients subconsciously develop rapport with me in a class or session. I have noticed that they seem to become happier and more joyful far quicker when I put myself in the highest positive vibration I can. Anything done communally is usually a more pleasant experience than if it were done alone. Communal joy is just as fulfilling and contagious. Decide to change your mindset from being obstructive to more objective and become in complete control of your thought processes. I have already said that **discipline** is fundamental for positive changes to happen. I want to show you how to make MASSIVE changes and take lasting and powerful steps towards making happiness happen routinely in your life...... I hope the meditations already covered have done this for you. Revisit them from time to time. From now on if you see an opportunity to feel happy pounce on it! Whether it is meeting a friend or watching a movie. **Pounce** on it like a hungry lion! I am not saying waste your time watching movies. But take time to create **happiness**, not think about the things you shouldn't or procrastinate. Be honest with yourself. Don't say you are busy if you are not! Make something of yourself. It is time to stop being so fragile and become the person you know you were predestined to be. Know your limits, but note that most people never push themselves even close to their true limit and end up with more limits thrust upon them.

Happiness Contemplation
Write a list of the things that make you happy and include them at any point you can. Use the diagram below to assist you.

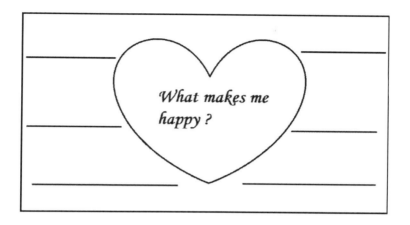

If you cannot meet your own demands, don't expect anyone else to!

Climbs & Struggles in life – Motivational text & Meditation with mantra/affirmations

What has your personal journey or climb in life been like so far? Have you navigated life with open or closed eyes? The only reason we move in a mundane manner is that the world does almost EVERYTHING for us. We tend to get carried by the demands of others. But this is not the real flow of the universe. Are you even present in your job? Or are you thinking about when you're going to get paid, a pay rise and when to go home to your family? Or when you will go out drinking with friends? Do you dread Monday mornings? I want to show you ways to **FIRE YOURSELF UP** and discover the true nature of who you are. Doing the things, you enjoy every day and looking deeply at the things you have not enjoyed each day will gently elevate your intuitive nature. Meditation needs to be streamlined according to what it is you want to achieve. Your state of mind needs to be as positive as possible. Perhaps having a poker face when that negative event happens and internally smiling at yourself for having kept your composure. Helping others can very often be your shortcut to **delight** and **happiness**. Have you helped anyone today? Have you gone the extra mile or just decided to help yourself? Being egotistic is part of our nature, but cultivating this single trait alone can lead to destruction and so too can the virtue of selflessness.

Always work on yourself **positively**. If you are stressed, bring your energy levels down first then positively motivate yourself in the right direction. Laughter is a good way to settle a troubled and tormented mind. So too is meditation, but know when to stop! Don't sit in meditation all day and fall asleep. And don't work yourself into the ground either. When you climb up to the top in one aspect of life, you can apply the tools you used to succeed in other areas. A famous Zen master once said, master one thing and you can master anything. Just apply the same techniques you used to succeed in other parts of your life. You can do it! Whatever area you believe to be challenging in your life, start to put your heart and soul into finding a resolution...whether it is completing an exam, getting a black belt, finding a life partner, overcoming an adversary or losing weight..... Find at least 12 ways to make **progress** and start to change that area and deploy them. If you are stressed, don't just meditate, you need a succession of ideas that become your meditation until you have resolved the issue of stress. Have an algorithm for change. For example, you might incorporate the following: drinking herbal tea every night, exercising, **meditating**, hypnotherapy, swimming, listening to **calming music**.

When you reach the destination of your climb and look down and see you all the people under each invisible breath you take...., you know success has happened in your own life, you understand completely that those who chose not to climb your metaphorical peak in life.....may have climbed others. You also believe your cross was huge and burdensome, yet there is no way you could know how difficult a climb might be for someone else, unless you want to reincarnate and live their life too. Perhaps those climbs they have made in were more important to them, more difficult and perhaps they transcended limits you may never exceed yourself. On the other hand, many dare not rise to the top in any area of their life. Fear cripples and restricts their every advance. There is always "something" that stands out in anyone who **choose**s NOT to flee the path they were destined to take. Those who walk any meaningful path of life have "COMPLETE **RAZOR-SHARP** CONVICTION" and "DISCIPLINE". I want to show you how to create energy of discipline and have the guts to push forward whatever the case. Maybe you already have this energy now, having read so far. Discipline is something frowned upon by many, because they see it as something negative or wish to stride through life effortlessly. Whether you are using the work hard or work smart route, there is much work to be done. I always strike a balance and face all my demons internally and externally.

In some way perhaps the climb for others has been very different and more difficult than yours. Perhaps you have plenty to learn from those individuals. I always speak to people who have achieved what it was I wanted to achieve. If I want to write books, I speak to people in my friend and business circle who have been successful in writing.

All people have much to contribute and **impart** useful information unknown to us, and perhaps the world. We all know this, but we sometimes underestimate some people and overestimate others. I always give everyone a listening ear, especially those who others shun. It is a good idea to open your ears and heart while listening to the life stories others tell, and absorb the positive learnings. Being alive and present in the moment, my friends, for me is in itself a dynamic, "in your face style" meditation. Living in the yogic way is taking time to listen to both the story of the homeless person and the person who is filthy rich. Both have a useful contribution.

Those who don't make climbs or have never chosen to, may need the encouragement to take things forward and to another level..... What is your name and what images come to the minds of people when they think of you? What images do you think come to their mind? I'm Paul Tavares and what defines me as a person is that I am always striving to exceed my potential. I am not perfect. Which human being is? I always do my best to help at least one or two people start their climb..... every day and I do. And when they get there, even if I have not **achieved** my own goal for that day, I feel as though I have achieved goals in a far bigger sense.

Perhaps there is someone who needs help from you along their climb. Or perhaps you need to be your own best friend today. The popular saying from Jesus Christ "Do unto others" can be applied to yourself too. If you do not treat yourself well and meet your own expectations, how can you do anything good for anyone else. Unconditional acts of love have been very rewarding for me. Why not help that someone unconditionally...? Especially when you yourself have had a bad day. Whoever that person might be.... Or maybe at this point in time you need to invest in yourself. That is, maybe you need to help yourself. If that is the case, do it wholeheartedly. To help others including yourself, to **develop** and **grow** in a beneficial way is like opening a gate for the energy of grace and character development. Perhaps you can start by helping someone on a similar journey to yourself.... but who is worse off... You can even do this by imparting information that has brought you to a stage they have not yet reached. You can give them a listening ear, a contact, proof read something, be moral support or offer a donation if you are in a position to. Not many extend a hand to **assist** another without expectation. Why not "be the change you wish to see" as Mahatma Gandhi said.

Affirmations are sentences, that work in profound ways to change the mind. But there are affirmations and affirmations. Some more powerful than others. The wording needs to be as positive as possible. And the way you say something, i.e. your tone, really matters. If you say something with the right energy behind it, you will feel the true power enriched within the word itself. If you cannot convince yourself of something, how can you think of **influencing** anyone else in the world. You can't. Words can encourage or destroy. Why not use words and self-talk to self-develop and not self-destruct. Your challenge might be to develop in a uniquely positive way, so be open to approaching problems in a way that is original. Whatever demands are put on you, you know what type of impact they have, so you need to find a way to function around them while you achieve all your goals in life. Always remember to approach your meditation with all your attention. You may need to modify what you are doing, perhaps decompose what you are doing in small mini-projects or tasks, even meditating for less time, in small bouts throughout the day, as a **viable** option, if you live, work and commute in environments that are very distracting.

Try the following exercise:

Find somewhere you will not be disturbed with a mirror. Close your eyes and think of someone you admire. Choose carefully. If you want physical strength, select someone who is physically strong. I always envision my hero **Bruce Lee (李小龙)** standing in horse riding stance as in the photograph below.

Select someone who has the **traits** you aspire to have... or a version of yourself who had the very traits that are missing in you now. Who is your hero? Remember aspiring to have something is never adequate enough. You MUST be **willing** to get it. Stop coming up with excuses and achieve your goals!

My Hero

Who is your hero? Think of someone you admire. Once you have thought through who this person might be. Imagine they are standing in front of you now. Take time to see every detail of how they might appear in the room with you. Imagine stepping into that person's body. Imagine what if would be like to have the same **strengths** that person has. How it would feel to have a body like theirs, if that is what you want. Perhaps it is what you want, that is if you want to attain only a certain level of physical strength. Perhaps you need to imagine what it is like to think very quickly, as they would. Or maybe be in complete control of a particular type of emotion or achieve a spiritual milestone/connection. Do this for a few minutes or so. Then open your eyes and as you **gaze** at yourself in a mirror. Look deeply into your eyes, like you are trying to connect with your own soul. I want you to now chant the following affirmations like a mantra. Say them aloud to the image of yourself in the mirror, like you are your hero giving yourself words of advice. Look deeply into your own eyes. It is said that the eyes are portals or the gateway to the soul itself. I want you to say each affirmation with complete conviction, certainty and **definitive positive energy**. Say each of them like you mean it. Not in a monotonal uncharismatic energy. Affirmations don't work that way! And even if you don't feel inspired, pretend you do. And act until you invoke and embody the energy you desire.

"MY MIND IS IN THE RIGHT STATE TO EFFORTLESSLY MANIFEST ALL THE POSITIVE THINGS I REQUIRE, EVEN GOOD THOUGHT PROCESSES" X10

"I ACHIEVE PHENOMENAL THINGS AND I USE THE ENERGY OF ABSOLUTE CONVICTION." X10

"I AM PHYSICALLY, MENTALLY, EMOTIONALLY & SPIRITUALLY STRONG AND I ENHANCE MY STRENGTHS EVERY DAY BY WORKING ON MY SELF DEVELOPMENT" x10

"I EASILY ELIMINATE ANY ACTIONS THAT ARE DESTRUCTIVE TO MYSELF AND THOSE AROUND ME" X10

"I ALWAYS THINK BIGGER AND BIGGER; I ACHIEVE MANY GREAT THINGS AND HELP TOUCH THE LIVES OF COUNTLESS PEOPLE" X10

"I CAN FOCUS EASILY; I AM TOTALLY ENGAGED IN ALL ASPECTS OF MY LIFE AND I FIND BEING PRESENT AN EASY TASK" X10

"I RECOVER FROM ANY SETBACKS EASILY AND ALWAYS ADVANCE IMMEDIATELY TOWARDS ALL MY GOALS" X10

You should also say the above as often as you can throughout your day silently in your mind. Especially if you feel depleted of **positive** energy. Sometimes people will pull you down through the comments they make. Not everyone will like you, you will not be everybody's cup of **tea**, but you should always LOVE YOURSELF!! I never let negative comments affect the real me. You should not allow negative comments to influence you either. Allow these powerful affirmations above and the words within to start resonating within you, be open to allowing them to make you feel better. Sometimes we are so closed and set on the idea that something will work and then our minds will not allow it to. When you are open and focused on being receptive you will start amassing the **energy** you require to manifest and evolve for the **better**.

Empowerment and empowering meditation exercise

I love to stand in the arms of nature and bask in the energy given to me by the creator. In Tai Chi this arm posture is a version of YinYang hands. Tai Chi is a martial art. This posture is a little like submission, but not weakness in submission. You could think of it as perhaps momentary deception like many forms of animal style Kung Fu. You can apply the Taoist philosophy, which Tai Chi is based upon, to all aspects of your life. Don't be stressed about the future, just trust in the power of creation and find a way to **positively** make it work for you and in others. If you do this diligently and perhaps learn something from the **creation** daily, one day you will look up and be surprised at how far you have come. I trust that all that is happening, is the way it should be happening and is evolving and unfolding the way it must. Do your part to the best of your ability, without resentment and let everything unfold according to the plan of God. To say it shouldn't be is like saying the creator's invention is flawed. I believe we are living in an intricate design we can never dream of understanding completely. Instead our role is to embrace creation and get on with creating what is good for the whole of humanity, other living beings and even the so-called inanimate world. I like to train and teach people... and to train alone. Training alone helps me to understand the nature of what is required by **nature** itself. I like to help others deal with negativity caused by depression, panic, anxiety, dismay and frustration. And I can proudly say I have. I like to help people become positive or at least carry on moving forwards even if one is not feeling great. It is easier to tell someone to **cheer up** than to help them.

I like to train alone too, sometimes, with absolutely nobody, not a human soul around me. I enjoy the lessons taught to me by my teachers of the past as I **reminisce**, those who have .... past ...and those still dwell in the present within the world of physical human animation. My most meaningful experience next to that presented by the creator is the delivery of insight endowed by nature herself and the powerful energy that creates all things. It is mindboggling to think that this same energy created all the remnants of the past and perhaps already those emerging in a predestined future. Love, respect and discipline come from a deeper understanding of the martial arts, **longevity** arts like Yoga and what transformative energy they truly hold. Practicing alternative and holistic therapeutic arts have further encouraged my push towards learning from mother nature. Each of the disciplines above steer us toward embracing nature. I like to always change and refine the work I do with people and make it better each time. Change and refinement is the essence of nature. Adapt or die. I hope this information can assist others to start to understand how to overcome the damaging obstacles in their life. Even if you do not practice any of the meditations and tasks I have enlisted, you can still gain much inspiration from just reading the text. I studied Japanese Karate in conjunction with many other martial arts. It taught me amazing emotional control. I learnt how to create aggression while fighting an opponent, then gentleness. Ultimately, it has taught me to manage my calm in extreme situations. If someone is going to punch you, most people freeze up these days. Karate has taught me amazing techniques.

I love Japanese culture and all it has to offer. If someone has never experienced intense levels of emotion, how can they think of advising others in how to control those emotions. In Karate, Kung Fu and Kalari, I have felt the fear of opponents, anger from getting hit, sadness from not meeting expectations and I learnt to **control** those **emotions** in the heat of battle. This mindset of a ninja has helped me tremendously. Karate opened many doors within the Japanese martial art world including Ninjutsu and energy martial arts. Symbolism is very powerful and in Japanese martial arts the triangle is considered a very powerful shape. It is the same shape you create when you make a fist with your hand, the knuckles form small triangles. The knees and elbows are also triangular at the edge. Noticing these subtle aspects in any mindful discipline is a way to bolster your intuitive nature. And discipline comes through practice, experience and noticing subtleties.

Try the following empowering breathing meditation that helps to still a troubled mind.

1.Sit **comfortably** and keep your hands on your lap elbows out. Sit somewhere outdoors if you can, where it is safe.

2. Keep your spine as straight as possible, you can keep it slightly **stretch**ed if you wish. But never strain.

3.Observe as much of anything in your ambient environment, with all your senses...any sounds...smells...sights...and anything you can **experience** around you. Do so for a couple of minutes. Perhaps you can start with one observation at a time or if you are an experienced meditator, try two or three.

4. Close your eyes and observe your inner world for a while, as widely as you can...in particular the activities of the mind itself....any feelings...sensations...thoughts....pictures in your mind's eye and music playing in your mind... is it something you can categorise easily? Open your eyes.

4. Now, look at the symbol below and try and see it in your mind's eye. Try and see it **clearly** in your imagination. Triangular objects, pyramids and stars have a powerful "focus friendly" energy.

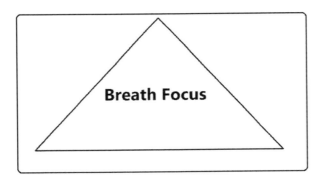

5. Then bring your **attention** specifically to the gentle movements that happen in your physical body... your heart beat and breathing rhythm.... any muscular twitching, perhaps even

the movement of blood within your body if you can really tune in at a deep level. Focus on one aspect of physicality at a time.

6. Finally focus on the feeling of your own **breath** alone. Don't control it, just observe it... its temperature, the sound and any smells the air pulls in and out of your body. Do this for a while. This will create the focus you require.

7. Now imagine a connection to anything in your environment that you observed. Think of one thing at a time. **Visualise** what it would be like to become a plant, insect, bird, cloud or even a part of a lake or river nearby. What would consciousness feel like? What would you want to say to the human version of yourself?

Do this daily and enrich yourself with the energy you need to face life in your best possible state and become a **positive** contributory element of life. We are all made of protons, neutrons and electrons. Science tells us that. And that everything is made of the same, including the chairs we sit on, so connecting to everything in meditation can be as easy a task as you want it to be. Every living and non-living element is an important part of the Rubik's cube of life.

WEIGHTLOSS MEDITATION & AFFIRMATIONS FOR DEVELOPING DISCIPLINE/CONTROL

People face a range of problems but often fail at weight loss or develop an eating disorder. My **advice** is, if you want to lose weight, you need to simply observe a balanced diet. This is essential for all modes of weight loss and weight gain and this is the most effective way you can lose weight slowly and safely. This is NOT a fob off. The normalisation process within your body will kick in only if you just commit to eating foods with good **nutritional value** for life. There are many other processes you can apply, but good nutrition is fundamental.

If you are overweight and if you want to seriously lose weight and get in awesome physical shape, then being committed is essential. As well as doing so safely and properly. Try intermittent fasting by all means, but not intermittent training with gaps of 'stocking up on carbs' and refined sugar. Also, you MUST understand what intermittent fasting is before trying it and make sure it is okay for you by checking with your physician... Fasting is never okay if you have an eating disorder. All people are different and you must make sure that as a person, this is okay for you. Keep focused on what is safe and keep on track!

Sometimes, our willpower is so weak that we need to recondition our mindset. Habit is something you need to develop. Make small but powerful changes with a goal to eat healthy always. Healthy eating, is not boring, you can eat sugary treats, but only after you have achieved **healthy** eating for a year, or otherwise, you are very likely to lapse back into bad eating **habits**. Try reading aloud the following text daily in order to give you the conviction you need to achieve your weight loss goals. Then meditate on the symbol further below.

"I am committed to losing weight safely by eating enough until I am full."

"I eat to sustain myself and not derive too much pleasure from just eating."

"I enjoy eating but I know my limit from now on."

"If someone upsets me or an adverse event comes my way, I find healthy ways to calm down. I still continue to eat foods for sustenance and I use any time I can to emotionally develop/strengthen myself."

"My goal is to be a healthy weight for my own body type then understand how to enjoy a few treats once I have attained my weight loss goal."

"I know I can achieve amazing results because if others can do it, so can I, so I **persevere**."

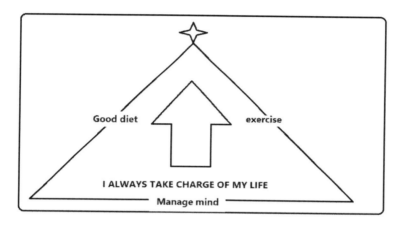

BULLYING, ASSERTIVENESS, MOTIVATIONAL TEXT & EMPOWERING EXERCISE

Anyone can change and the very nature of the world we live in is changing all the time. There is a saying in the world of evolutionary genetics, "adapt or die", if you do not adapt, you will not survive. Nature naturally eliminates any and all things that are not **robust** enough to survive. Yes, being a better person in life can sometimes mean being humble. This can work. But sometimes you need to stand up for yourself if evolution requires you to do so. **Adaptation** can mean finding strength. If you always "let things go" you can be doing yourself a lot of injustice and if you tackle a problem you could also be creating more. So, what should you do? Make a quick decision. Do not sit on the fence. Yes, rise above those who want to pull you down...but don't let them rise above you and crush you in the process. If you keep getting struck down by a particular person, rising above them in a noble way can only happen by taking the **energy** of courage. Man up! Tell them how you feel! You have to tackle the bully like a virus. As a former scientist, I have studied how viruses replicate for many years and published many articles on them including on HIV and prions (infectious proteins). Viruses are difficult to eliminate because they keep changing and evolving. And the nuclear arms race between scientists developing medication and microbial adaptation is constantly being lost to nature and the superbugs it produces. Though a virus is a tiny subcellular parasite, it changes rapidly and even the immune system itself has a hard time finding ways to eliminate these **ever-evolving** parasites.

Mimic both macroscopic and microscopic nature to solve your problems in life. Change your approach all the time, like a virus. You will find the right way to tackle any situation including a bully in the workplace or at school. The faster you change and modify your approach, the more successful you are likely to be. I have seen that most situations involving any form of harassment requires a marriage of both the energy of **compassion** and **assertiveness**, whether at work, college or school. Keep your focus on the behaviour and never start getting personal. As the more mature individual, whenever you interact with a bully, you should put boundaries in place in the future, so you don't sink to the other persons level. Don't sink to this worm's level and believe me, anyone watching your interaction with this person, will know in their mind you are a true champion of life. We are all actors in life. You need to own the stage of your life, be your own hero and support your own cause. Bullies are narcissistic and they will rarely respond to a plea to stop. They draw on the energy of vulnerability because this is what they themselves feel. They wish to attract this energy for their own empowerment. In fact, they will suck out all your energy if you hand them power, if you start begging them to stop bullying you with victimised energy, they will continue to.

Use **assertiveness**! Remember the time is now, not at the end of your life after being a doormat for any Tom, Dick or Harry. Be assertive now, find the courage or animal nature in you and use it to drive you. If you have trouble with that, I can help you out. Again, do not....let anyone bully you, whether they are richer, stronger or scarier than you! Never be a doormat for anyone!

Try the following empowering meditation.
1. Start to focus on your natural breathing pattern
2. Imagine a time when you felt you achieved something, whether small or large.
3. See yourself achieving whatever it is you did. Search for any positive sensations in your body while you picture this achievement in your mind's eye.... like it is displayed on a screen in your mind. **Observe** your body language and if you find that difficult to do, see yourself standing tall and strong.
4. If you cannot think of yourself confidently, then imagine someone you look up to. Perhaps a hero from a movie or even a childhood hero from a cartoon.
5. Reach out with your hands and with **complete** belief pull into yourself the strength from the screen of that image into your own physiology. Use your imagination or actually reach out and grab the power from this energy form. Crazy as it seems it works. **Trust** me, I have used these techniques myself and I have faced my share of bullies.

6. Now picture the bully standing directly in front of you. Imagine they are much smaller than they are in reality...like they have shrunk three times smaller. Think of them as a child who does not understand right from wrong. Say to yourself. I am very calm and I can think quickly and clearly. When I am around this person, I am able to use my interaction with them as an opportunity to develop courage to stand up for myself. And do what is right for me as a person. Imagine there is much you need to impart to this person who themselves needs guidance in a world that has not given them the opportunity to evolve for their better good.
7. Lastly in your mind hear and see yourself having a conversation and easily coming to a resolution.

Remember my friend's, **self-improvement or development** is the only way to engage positively with life. This must be a consistent and ongoing process, because anything that evolves to survive in the world we live in, is always **adapting** and **changing** for the better.

DEVELOP MIND & BODY FLEXIBILITY – TAICHI STYLE EXERCISE FOR RELAXING THE BODY AND ENHANCING FLEXIBILITY AND RESPONSIVENESS

I love the word flexibility. I think it is important to have a flexible nature in an ever-changing world. You must do all that you can to **achieve** your goals in life. HOWEVER, make sure you adopt a mature flexible approach if your energies are diverted by some unforeseeable event. The **flow of life** may not always correlate with your "small plan" in the way you think it should. Regaining strength & flexibility when I sustained a serious knee injury was a difficult task especially when many professionals had a very inflexible approach. I went through an **emotional** roller-coaster and my mindset itself needed to be flexible because it was stretched in many different directions, but my end goal remained the same. And I successfully drove the vessel filled with emotion to my end destination, that is, I **rehabilitated** myself. As a **wellbeing** expert, I have to be very flexible because my students and clients come from all walks of life and have various different requirements. So, this requires me to constantly **adapt** what I teach and how I deliver information to others. I have adapted many of the physical, mental and spiritual exercises I have taught to others to rehabilitate myself too. Everyone is on their own unique journey through life and has their own **challenges** so make sure the techniques you use from this book are beneficial in terms of your **requirements** as a person.

In life itself the martial & Tai Chi approach has always been to mimic nature. The birds, animals and plants grow and develop in the best way they can. However, when a hurricane or natural disaster comes, they do their best to survive in any way possible and if they cannot they rebuild what they have lost straight away. They submit to what they cannot control but use submission to build something more **powerful**, perhaps they have more insight into God's plan or the flow of the universe than any human being can ever dream of having. Learn to flow like the wind or water.... that is.... be willing to change direction to get to where you need to be... if it is clear you must and even if your end destination is not completely **clear** you must survive. Everything in this world and the universe seems to be in a state of constant flux and cycles.

My son is eight years old and his theory, is that "the world is like the human body in so many ways. Volcanic eruptions, hurricanes and earthquakes are a little like involuntary responses in our own bodies when we are out of balance." Perhaps he is right. Perhaps this is the Earth's natural mechanism of control. I also believe our bodies are like mini **energy** worlds that go through cycles, just the same as anything we observe in the universe. Even those who I have spoken to who have experienced some form of past life regression seem to notice patterns in the cycles which they encountered in former lives. And, even if the experience was completely one within the mind and nothing **metaphysical**, it is still an experience that can lead to a realisation of how to escape a particular cycle of destruction in life. We can push our bodies and minds to change in a more beneficial way if we employ certain techniques that encourage gravitation towards a new positive purpose. Perhaps towards the realisation of our life's purpose. Your life purpose is ultimately determined by the way you behave and act. However, certain behaviours can make the journey a little easier.

Learning from nature is one of the most powerful things you can do. Rocks that sit in a stream will eventually get broken by the current, but those that go with it will roll into beautiful smooth pebbles. **First-hand** learning by being in natures arms as much as you can will teach you a flexible and adaptive approach to almost anything. If an insect or bird loses a leg, they find another way to move and recreate what they do not have. This is not something we can teach each other. What is commendable is if a human can do that too and have the emotional and mental strength to continue. I can think of so many **inspirational** people who actually have. To be flexible is to do what is required, perhaps in a way that is different and unique to you. In the moment, do what you can to overcome a difficult situation, move your body around any obstacles, change your path momentarily to be on the same path and set your mind on the **right** track. Whatever "right" means to you.

Everyone has the **potential** to **express** themselves in a unique and **beautiful** way. I have been studying "Tai Chi" for a long time and I too have my own variation based on several styles. There are five major Tai Chi forms. I liked many of the methods including the Yang and Chen form and many forms of Qi Gong. I found I wanted to express them in a way that felt better for me as a person. For me Tai Chi, Qi Gong and other internal arts are ways to express the **mind, body, emotion** and **spirit**. Whether it is as a martial art, health discipline or energy art. After years of practice, I created my own way to express the forms, which felt good for me and the many devotees I teach. I would suggest you test many different styles and find one you like that is suitable for you. Try the following activity, it is my variation of the Tai Chi move withdraw and push, it can be done seated and standing:

1. Stretch your arms forward in line with your shoulders, palms facing down.
2. Inhale bringing your hands in towards your body.

3. Exhale as you drop them a little and push them forward and point your palms away from your body as you push.
4. Slow the movement down.
5. Align your movement with your breathing.
6. Breathe from the lower portion of the lungs, sometimes called belly breathing, although it is more correctly lower lung breathing which fills the whole of the lung.

Do this slowly and steadily over and over... this is the essence of Tai Chi for **health**. Though I teach many different forms, Yang, Chen etc... the above is designed for a complete beginner or those who just want to get going and receive the **benefits** of Tai Chi immediately. I teach short and long forms, 108 forms etc. But I also teach modified versions of forms and I like to **adapt** what I do according to what is required by those I teach. If Tai Chi mimics nature, then it should be able to evolve, just as everything else in this world does.

In my experience, you can create **amazing** levels of calm and contentment using just a few very simple yet powerful Tai Chi style exercises. The first forms developed were actually around 10 or 12 moves in length and the simple 24 forms taught in gyms are very easy to learn. When I teach, I use forms I have created on my own through experimentation. I have created these shortened versions of forms simply so that students can begin practicing straight away. These forms are sometimes parts of the long form but mostly unique versions of what I believe this age of people require. If you want to learn Tai Chi for self-defence, practicing one move over and over, thinking of a suitable application and testing it in your class can be the best way to excel in that area. The self defence applications can assist a practitioner in developing in terms of **visualisation**, although martial arts are not taught this way until you reach a deeper level of understanding. You can use the tried and tested applications which I will save for another book and in my classes, but it is also good to evolve and try things that are different to add a new dynamic to this **amazing** art. Perhaps you can create your own unique martial art. You can test new moves with your comrades, just as the amazing Bruce Lee did and ultimately went on to develop one of the most **powerful** martial arts, **jeet kune do**.

TUNING INTO TODAY – CONTROLLED BREATHING AND SAMPLINGING THE ENERGY OF TODAY

Getting in tune with the **energy** of each day sets us up long term to become more in tune with natural flows of energy and ultimately all that exists.... Many experts of **mind, body, emotion and spirit** disciplines will tell you to embrace nature in order to become a calmer and **grounded** individual. But if you want to think even deeper about this, think of everything both inside and outside of you as an extension of yourself. And try to understand everything and everyone at its deepest level. Don't be spoon fed by what the world has told you, be curious and discover the world for yourself.

I love Yoga and the deeper understanding it brings to our world. It is not "just nature" you need to align yourself with. Yoga means union. But think of Yoga in terms of '**union**' or 'oneness' with everything natural and unnatural ... it is unionisation with everything animate, inanimate, **natural** and man-made. Perhaps our constructs are no more unnatural than anything else. The only unnatural thing about us is that we consciously cause alienation and brand everything in some abnormal way. All that we experience around us exists as an interconnected network with a wider purpose.

On a very large level through telescopes and other optical devices we see the flow as spiralling orbits of planets, comets and galaxies. The moon, the sun, the other stars in distant solar systems and everything at a macroscopic level is all an intermingling mass of energy like a big YinYang symbol with dimensions of darkness and light. This energy is also in a state of evolution and flux with one type turning into another, just like water in a vessel finding its level. **Science**, supports this view and understanding of energy and how it is constantly changing into different forms. Both **order** and disorder exist within our universe and everything in it, including the extension we call the human body. This is the true nature of meditation. It is set out to control the different dimensions of the body in order to create better unity between them. It is usually the thought processes in the mind that are many times out of control. Many Yoga systems I have been trained in teach that acknowledging thoughts and mind processes is the best way to create **calm**. Ignoring thoughts and grinding them away can help short term but like someone who wants to be heard, they may come back and trouble you. You need to understand what it is you are trying to **control** in order to control it. Stop hiding from what you most fear. Understanding the types of thoughts within your mind will assist you in controlling the thought processes that create emotions thereafter.

At the deepest spiritual level, being aware of the algorithms of nature and its natural cycles is one way to become synchronised with the flow of the universe. Open your **mind** to the possibility of becoming aligned with the universal flow or **God's plan**. Perhaps you need to open a window first thing and take in a breath of air. Take in the energy of the day and let it set you in line with the flow of the day. Maybe you need to open the energy window to your heart and place yourself in someone else's position in order to

embrace and understand them better. Sample some of the energy outside, whether it is by breathing it in through an open window or intuitively calling someone you feel you should. This is one reason why many martial artists and yogi's practice outdoors first thing in the morning or upon awakening. The sun can give you a hint of what is to come if you bask in its energy first thing, it can even give you the energy to deal with what you may face later on. Many ancient devotees knew the power of awakening early and basking in the rays of the sun. Sun salutation can help to accelerate the process of understanding universal flow and absorption of beneficial energy.

Try the following meditation to connect with faint noncorporeal energies around you:

1. Sit outdoors at sun rise or sun set when the heat is not too strong. Sit **comfortably** and become aware of your natural breathing rhythm.
2. Start to control your breathing by inhaling slowly and deeply filling your lungs from the lower belly up to your collar bone.
3. Make sure you do not overfill your lungs as this itself can stretch them and cause much discomfort.
4. As you **breathe** in try to become aware of the energies from the outer world... Then just focus on any minor energies. Not just the rays from the sun, the light energy from the sky, clouds. And feel the process of any subtle energies entering and filling the different cells in your body..... and as you release the air from your body, I want you to try attuning your body at the microscopic level, and macroscopic level..... and try synchronising with any energies entering and leaving your body. Some of the energy that enters your body will feel **beneficial** and pleasant, others may not. You are a semi-contained energy vessel with inward and outward flows of energy. And it is this flow that encourages synchrony with all that exists in the outer universe. **Embrace** this!

5. As you control your breathing this way, you also feel like the breathing pattern itself is creating a calming effect within, like the gentle rhythm of the ocean waves on a beach. In partaking this process, you will develop a deeper connection with nature and the energy that resides within the never-ending dimensions of what we call reality.
6. Return to observing your **normal** breathing pattern and observe your own normal natural breathing rhythm for a while.

EASY CHI GONG EXERCISE FOR RELIEVING STRESS & LOOSENING THE JOINTS IN THE ARMS

Tai Chi and Chi Gong can be **practiced** almost anywhere. Chi Gong or Qi Gong is an exercise system that pre-dates even Tai chi. Like dance, practice is something a devotee must undertake to make sure the **movement**s are perfect. But Tai Chi and Chi Gong are not only practiced for their beautiful slow meditative like movements. The moves have specific health and martial applications.

Practice is **fundamental** and mastery can disappear just as quickly as it was acquired. Some practice every day is better than a two hour stretch once a week. Where you practice is not important, as long as you do. As long as you do some practice, indoor or outdoor is absolutely fine. You can always adapt the exercises in such a way that you can even practice movement in a tiny box room. On my own Chi Gong journey, I have noticed that going outdoors in the early morning hours helps a devotee create **discipline** and appreciate the interplay of one's inner energies as they intermingle with outer influences of nature. Try to train outdoors at least some of the time, so as to experience the difference between the two extremes. A true Taoist monk might try both to create balance between energy inside and outside. If you cannot train outside due to whatever constraints exist for you, indoors is better than not at all. Perhaps open a window while you

train. The word balance is something worth holding in your mind while practicing anything related to longevity and a wonderful mantra to hold in your heart.....

I sometimes practice Tai Chi style arm movements from A stationary standing position. You can still derive much benefit from doing Tai Chi movements from a stationary position. Many Chi Gong exercises, are practiced a little like this. Chi Gong is an energy exercise created by Taoist devotees in China that involve using the body and mind to channel real **energy**.

Try the following **exercise**. Imagine you are swimming, use your arms to push forwards and out like a swimming style exercise. It is a little like the breast stroke, but with the palms facing down towards the floor. This particular exercise helps to **loosen** the joints and slowly erodes away stress and also helps the body build up its levels of Earth **prana**, **chi** or **qi**.

1. Sit or stand and place one foot in front of the other.
2. Keeping your shoulders relaxed and holding your hands out with your palms facing the floor as in the picture below, make circular **movement**s like you are swimming.
3. Make certain that you keep your palms facing the floor, I cannot stress enough the importance of doing this.
4. **Breathe** in as you open your chest and breathe out as you bring your hands back towards your body.
5. Imagine your hands are creating friction with the molecules in the air and as a result charging up your body with chi.

Perhaps this breathing pattern is counterintuitive to that of a swimmer, but you will soon get used to it and feel the true benefit of this exercise at so many different levels. If it does not resonate with you, breathe in a way which does. Perhaps you should breathe in as you pull in towards your body and out as you push forward and to the sides. Or just breathe normally, but visualise the **creation** of friction without **physical** tension.

Longevity through using martial arts

Information relating to martial arts and some higher-level yogic practices, was kept secret in ancient times for fear that it would be misused. Authentic Tai Chi, Karate, Yoga, Kalari, **meditation** and other wellbeing or **empowering** modalities, can be defined in many ways. I look at these **discipline**s as a way to transcend normal human ability.

These disciplines change the structure of the body and it becomes extremely strong. After much practice, the body can even become capable to store vast amounts of **energy** and integration between the mind, body and emotions becomes more intimate. Mental response and inbuilt reactions happen at super human speed. Here is a routine you can try that demonstrates the above.

1. Stand in a high horse-riding stance as in the picture below.

2. **Focus** on your natural breathing rhythm for a while.
3. Feel the air as you breathe in and out as a physical attribute first.
4. Feel its temperature and the volume it inhabits in your lungs.
5. **Imagine** drawing in strength & stability as you inhale.
6. Imagine the energy of strength and stability surging up into your body from the ground into your legs and entire body.
7. Let that strength fill your whole body, as though it were hollow. You have to imagine this process first in order to experience it.
8. As you feel the surge of energy, shift your **attention** to the outside world.
9. Listen to the sounds around you.
10. Look carefully at everything. Look at each of the colours in everything around you.
11. Try to determine if certain natural colours have a more positive effect on your mind than others.
12. Close your eyes and **imagine** your body is covered with the colours that nurture you in a positive way.

13. Imagine those colours filling all the cells in your body and bask in the moment for as long as you wish.

MEDITATION AND Qi GONG/YOGA STYLE EXERCISES FOR MENTAL EMOTIONAL & PHYSICAL BALANCE (Coordination & Locomotion)

I worked in the numerous scientific industries for many years and pharmaceutical industry for over five years in clinical research. Medication for a particular disease must be taken to either cure or control it. Regular **meditation** can also have a very powerful effect on the biochemical and emotional mix within the body. So can any change you make, whether it is a behaviour, exercise and spirituality. I believe that regular practice of meditation is **fundamental** for any level of control over yourself.

Just as some medicines can have an adverse effect on the **biochemistry** within some individuals and perhaps lead to an allergic reaction, some meditations can be unsuitable for some and like a **miracle** cure for others. I have led many different meditation groups including popular **mindfulness meditation**, which unbeknown to me, I naturally practiced very often in childhood. The only thing is at that time it was called Za Zen or Zen meditation. This was a form that I found very enjoyable indeed. It was my favourite type of meditation and still is along with standing and walking meditation or Kinhin. One could argue that many forms of meditation are types of mindfulness and mindfulness is a very broad term for the vast majority of meditation forms that exist in the west. Remember, the present does not really exist and time is merely a way in which we choose to **comprehend** a world we find difficult to understand. In my view full awareness of everything around and inside us is better than thinking of the present if we want to deepen our understanding of what we want to achieve.

Standing still and completely motionless in meditation is one of the best ways to settle the mind quickly. As a child, each year, I actually noticed a shift in my level of consciousness as my awareness became sharper. Perhaps because I meditated routinely. Or perhaps as we **grow** and develop there is a natural process that brings about this change. I think my awareness consciously helped me to see the **transition** in my evolution. I was completely aware of this process. I would practice the mountain pose as a child, to focus and discipline my mind and take that shift to another level or back to a level where I felt stillness. The mountain pose is perhaps the simplest looking pose, but this is far from true. It not only strengthens the body; it helps power the mind and all the dimensions that make a human who they are. I would sometimes vary the pose and stand motionless with my arms out stretched to the sides or stretched backwards. In each position I would notice a slightly different sensation emotionally and physically at the internal level. A small variation in my arm position seemed to **invoke** a very different type of **energy**. I would practice this type of meditation standing motionless for minutes in the beginning and initially I found it boring. However, something kept drawing me back to this practice. I didn't feel dissuaded and I built up my stamina to levels that allowed me to stay standing for much longer, with my arms out stretched. Thereafter, I never missed a day of practice, regardless of how I felt. I was determined to take something beneficial out of this process, it gave me **endurance**, **courage** and I decided to continue for no real reason other than to experiment with the technique on myself.

I had no idea I was practicing a refined version of yogic mountain pose, a very popular way to start a Hatha Yoga session in India. This meditative pose probably evolved into what is now called Zhan Zhaung. Zhan Zhaung was a creation of the ancient Chinese and is a practice that is often coupled with many Tai Chi or Tai Ji styles and **Qi** Gong, although in the west it is still quite new and not so well integrated into practices. I used similar postures to steady my mind. I recognised what I was doing as an almost spontaneous recreation straight away when one of my Chinese Kung Fu teachers started to show me classic Zhan Zhaung postures. He confirmed my **practice** was indeed a type of Zhan Zhaung meditation. In the photograph below, I am practicing a pose called hugging the tree or standing still like a post. This is perhaps the most common Zhan Zhaung exercise in **circulation** outside China.

I use my version, the Yoga mountain pose and what this master taught me to develop my own still **meditation postures** and create something that really worked for me. They became a fusion of all the knowledge I have accumulated from the Chinese, Japanese and Indian martial/peaceful disciplines I have studied.

If you practice any version at all, you will find that after building your stamina, the ability to stay still and motionless while observing the breath and thoughts will become easier and easier. Your body will become more receptive to energy as it does in the practice of hatha Yoga, still prayer, meditation and other forms that ultimately illicit channelling of very powerful energy.

Your **skeletal, muscle and organ systems** within you will function far better than before. Perhaps your relationship and rapport with them will also become more greatly enhanced, as mine has. Your energy levels are certain to sky rocket and you will be able to direct energy coherently, creating for yourself better health.

In the picture below, I am practicing a standing martial stance called cat stance or empty stance. This is not mountain pose or Zhan Zhaung, this is a traditional way to train in ancient Kung Fu or Gong Fu styles and one of the ways in which my teachers taught me the basics of the **animal forms.**

Standing in a stance and breathing or training in arm movements was a preferred way to practice in ancient times. You can gain all the benefits of Zhan Zhaung through practicing in this way and in one of many stances.

I like to train my balance physically by dropping my weight onto my back leg as in the picture and holding this stance for a good 20 minutes at least. Holding the pose for this length of time will create feelings of self-worth and the energy of endurance. For those of you who practice **karate,** another style which I have enjoyed practicing for many years, this is a little like back stance. And I would encourage holding back stance as an alternative to **cat stance**. Wake up early and try standing like this for a couple of minutes, then gradually extend your time. Use the back of a chair if you are not used to balancing.

For balance of mind and physical balance try the following.

1. Stand in the position in the picture above and use a chair to support yourself if necessary.
2. Sink down to a comfortable level on your back leg so you are not in any discomfort or off balance in any way.
3. Hold the leg and arm position or modified arm position for as long as you can.
4. Just observe all that is around you, as well as your thoughts and your breath while remaining still as you can.
5. Repeat this daily for a week and see how settled your mind becomes. You will also find your balance becomes better as your body adapts and becomes more comfortable with the process.
6. Reduce your time or stop for a day or so in-between if you need a rest...but at least do a minute of breathing meditation as a substitute if you decide to take a break.

Anxiety Meditation & dousing the body for tension

If you can go into meditation itself in a calmer more relaxed state of mind, you will benefit tremendously. How can you keep yourself calm before meditation in order to get the most from it? If you are naturally highly strung or you are experiencing something very stressful in your life, try drinking an herbal tea, listening to some calming music then watching a comedy. Preparation can be so beneficial.... now try the following meditation.

1. Sit or lie down in a comfortable place where you won't be distracted.

2. Then focus as best you can on the present and keep your eyes open reading and following the instructions below.

3. Scan your body for areas that are tense starting either from the top of the head to the toes or from the toes to the top of the head. Take your time doing this. If you find tension in a particular place, say the word **relax** moving your body a little as if to shake off the tension. If it does not subside it does not matter, what does matter is the suggestion.

4. Then stretch and tense all your muscle groups one at a time in the following way.

5. Start with the feet, curl the toes round towards the soles of your feet and create tension and stretching for a few seconds, then release the tension. Stretch your toes, move them around.

6. Then move onto the legs. Tense the leg muscles for a few seconds, then **relax**. Bend your legs a few times gently.

7. Tense the shoulders by bringing your shoulders up towards the sides of your face and relax.

8. Tense your forehead by frowning for a few seconds and relax the tension.

9. Sit in the posture I have adopted in the picture above if you can comfortably, knees open and fists on hips for a few minutes. Just enjoy sitting peacefully and observing the natural rhythm of your breath.

YINYANG MEDITATION
This meditation is powered by the energy of intent. It works a little like advanced level **Tai Chi**. When a Tai Chi or **Chi Gong** practitioner attains a certain level of skill, they are able to channel Chi with the very thought of bringing it into the body. The arms are merely tools of faith to pull in and invoke real energy.

If you discipline your mind to the extent that you can focus it completely on what you want to do, you should be able to **experience** this effect. I always recommend that channelling exercises like this are done after some physical Tai Chi or Yoga because the in surge of energy can happen very fast and can also be a very intense experience. Getting used to the energy first is, in my opinion, advisable.

Yoga postures and Tai Chi movements are stage by stage
 for a specific reason. Create your own way as a master by all means but remember that you have to be physically strong enough to hold high levels of energy. Mental strength is necessary for physical strength and both are fundamental for emotional strength. Aligning with these three principals in unity with the external information feed from the universe, is necessary to safely experience the deepest levels of **spirituality**.

Read through the steps below then try them to experience **deep**er levels of understanding in yourself. I have included a picture to help you to deepen your understanding of the process. By being aware of the interplay of opposite energies, you can gain much insight. **True** awareness should be like a light coming out of nowhere and illuminating the darkness of your present understanding.

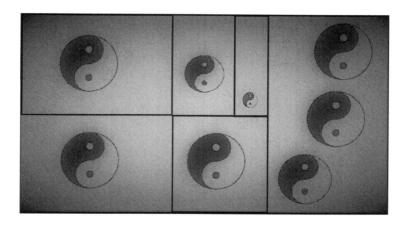

1. Sit **comfortably**.

2. Imagine you are attached strongly to the earth or rooted to the ground by feeling it with your feet and shoes. Like a tree or plant. Keep your awareness on the ground and feel a strong and deep connection with the Earth.

3. Imagine the energy from the planet is climbing up and into your body from imaginary roots extending out of your feet into the core of the **planet**.

4.Then focus on any real feelings, like tingling. Perhaps the energy is travelling further up into your body. Perhaps right up into your head. If you cannot experience this, imagine it is slowly creeping up into the upper layers of the body until it does reach the head. Now think of the rays of the sun. Imagine this energy from our sun entering your crown and feel the energy streaming through your head and the rest of your body. Perhaps you can imagine this white light entering the sky, turning yellow then slowly sifting through the gas molecules in the air and into your head. Let the two energies intermingle. Feel for the sensation of unconscious mixing between the two energies and any others that live in your body. Do they feel good or not so beneficial?

5. Think of the many symbols of YinYang in the image above and the energy in your body as a **functional** interplay of many opposites

that are opposing and evolving. Much like everything in this world. The two complimentary yet opposing energies are something to embrace.

6 Feel for a fusion of the many energies and experience any sensations within yourself. Write them down in a journal and look at your notes after you have completed several meditations of this kind.

PRESENCE & MEDITATION

Self-awareness as well as being aware of all that is around you is essential to live a meaningful and fulfilled life. **Awareness** is often something thrust upon us in the face of dangers. Often, heightened awareness can be created when we experience the ultimate level of happiness too! So perhaps these experiences teach us that in order to be focused on the present we either require that our bodies are exposed to an extreme level of adversity or the opposite. And, thereby become **awakened**. However, there are many slow steady roots to awakening that work to slowly coax the mind into such a state.

Enlightenment and awakening are not always the objective others wish to reach. Your goals spiritually, may be very different from someone else's who just wishes to exist and live their life. **Mindfulness** is currently the most popular form of meditation in the UK at the moment. It teaches a student how to create more awareness. Awareness of everything including thoughts, brings about a certain level of control through altering the nature through which we respond to the world. Direct control of thoughts and other functions within you is possible, but not without practice.

We can **PASSIVELY** and **ACTIVELY** force positive impressions into our minds thereby develop our positive nature more quickly. Negative images filtering into the mind can be overwhelmed or diluted by positive imagery. That is why being outside in nature with its positive vibe and unique blend of mood enhancing colours and imagery is therapeutic for the mind. Any positive imagery can settle the most troubled mind. Let nature provide the presentation slides you feed into your mind for calm and clarity and to further instil positivity in you.

Try the following and treat it as an all-day meditation

Consciously add specific **positive thoughts** and imagery into your mind every ten minutes. Perhaps set a timer to remind yourself to feed positive thoughts into your mind every 10 minutes.

If you are not feeling so positive and you are in a "very dark place", believe me the pain will pass. Just remember you are not alone, there are people going through a worse or similar situation. You need to face whatever it is that is causing you that pain! In the **martial art** world, I remember, the only time I started growing and getting better was when I started to face the people in clubs, I feared the most. Imagine facing that which you most fear and just feel the relaxation that follows. The **energy** of pain can be converted into something more beneficial and will soon take the path of relaxation and bliss if you are open to this happening.

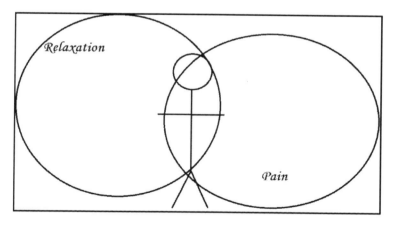

We need to face our demons, understand what we fear most and why we do in order to feel **peace** and **relaxation** of mind.

The vast majority of us live in a state of reactiveness. If something happens, we immediately react to it. A negative response might be a motorist who manoeuvres their car in a dangerous way, which immediately puts you in "fight or flight" mode or makes you retaliate in some way. Unknowingly many people control our emotional responses through their actions. It is possible to create **positive reactivity**. The world would be a better place if people stopped letting little things "get to them".

Just as a snake will strike out and bite anything that crushes its tail, whether it was an accident or not, we also respond like this the less enlightened and more primitive we are. If we learn to control these animal-like responses, we can certainly develop ourselves and perhaps society into a group of people that cooperate in a way that is **beneficial** for all. Dominion over yourself is not a bad thing. Strive to dictate the way you feel through power meditation and taking action to create a state of mind you wish to have! This can eliminate uncontrolled action and negative decline. Although fire flickers it "knows" to control its spread and moves only through what it can burn and consume.

Being devoted to become better in all ways is attained by maximising all opportunities and taking in positive energy any time you can. Whether that energy comes from the natural world, music you enjoy or **healthy** organic home-grown foods does not matter. The chakras or energy vortexes and meridians or energy lines within the body are filled with free-flowing energy when we adopt positive practices.

Try the following meditation
1. Imagine the crown of your head is magnetized such that is can pull energy directly into it. Visualise what pulling energy might feel like and imagine this effect from the **crown** of your head through your spine and towards your tail bone.
2. Do the same for the 6 remaining **energy** centres or chakras. Starting at the chakra itself. The 6th chakra is in the centre of the forehead, the 5th around the throat, the 4th on the heart centre, the

3rd solar plexus, 2nd below the belly button and finally the 1st at the base of the spine. In reality there are many more, but let us understand these first. Cleansing happens when you are more open to the practice itself and if you have a little faith.

Mindfulness meditation aims to concentrate your attention and evoke the power of **relaxation** and **focus**. It can successfully free practitioners of stress and the ailments stress brings. It is a useful preliminary tool in your journey to **harmonise** the body. But ultimately it aims to **cultivate** another level of development. You can cultivate real energy or chi at the etheric level only when you are aware of it.

In the picture above, I am enjoying a deep meditation. I have always meditated, and I really enjoy developing a better understanding of how I work as a **multifaceted** human being. Never feel that it is a must to practice mindfulness. When I meditate, whilst in deeply composed state, I leave the **sensory** world briefly. My 5 senses cease to exist, my breathing pattern is very slow and I experience an amazing understanding or what the yogis call union.

Try the following meditation for a similar experience.

1. Imagine watching yourself from a distance. Imagine you are like an insect sitting on a wall observing yourself as in the picture below.

2. Now imagine you are both the insect and yourself simultaneously. Take a bit of time to feel the split. Become the two beings in your mind's eye, that is, the insect and the human form. Imagine controlling your physical self from a distance.

3. Imagine you can control yourself like you would a character in a computer game.

4. This interesting process will help you to detach from any negative feelings you hold within, as well as reactive responses you may have had if you were completely attached to that which you currently identify as yourself. From this place, imagine a typical day and the situations and people you encounter. Observe what or who you are reacting to **positively** and negatively. What were you enjoying and not enjoying so much? What is positive is subjective and must be something you truly enjoy and not something you think you should enjoy.

5. Go about your day to day tasks but every so often, use this remote viewing style technique to enhance your perception of yourself and all you **interact** with.

Be Compassionate & COMPASSION MEDITATION

Create compassionate energy picturing all people as family or **loved ones** before each interaction with them. If you make this a regular practice, you will relate far better to people and become a more positive experience in their lives. Animals instinctively tune into **subtle energies** and are far more **compassionate** in many different ways. An animal will only kill if it feels threatened or hungry and is perhaps fully in tune to how the energies of this world must be used. As higher beings of this world, surely, we should be completely attuned to subtle energies. These are the energies that reside in the world we live in. Animals are amazing. I have learnt so much from the natural world and vastness of life accumulated in this sphere of **dynamic energy flow** we call home.

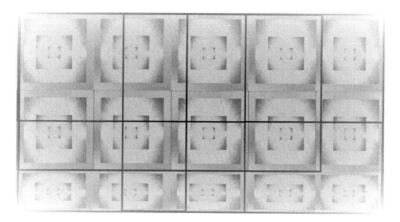

1. Each day think of 5 people who have either done wrong to you or that you are not **close** to. Think of what unconditional love feels like for you and imagine sending that **love** to those people perhaps by closing your eyes and sending them a **loving embrace**. As if they are as close to you as a family member.

2. Imagine sending them unconditional love in the form of true sincere **compassion**, like you are radiating loving white light to them or whatever colour of light love represents for

you. Perhaps wish them the energy for positive success, without expecting this energy to return to you in some way.

3. Use the image above and imagine sending this light out from your heart centre to all these people, like little light extensions **emanating** from your body.
4. Finish by holding the image of emerging light, just as in the picture, in your mind's eye. Open your eyes very gently and relax this way for a minute.

Energy exercise for feeling subtle energy and healing

1. Hold your hands out straight with the thumbs and index fingers touching each other creating a triangular shaped gap with your hands.
2. Look through the triangle at the air within the 2D shape you have created and **simultaneously** out into the distance.
3. Then change your hand position so that your palms face one another and keep them around an inch of so apart. See if you can sense a push, pull, tingling or heat between your hands.
4. Whatever sensation you experience, tune into anything that feels outside the spectrum of your normal five senses. Once you feel something, try to tune yourself into the experience more by envisioning the same sensation in other parts of your body that require attention. By envisioning this process, you start to attract a more beneficial **energy** into

yourself unknowingly. To use this energy for healing, you can employ an ancient technique called laying of hands by simply placing your hands on any part of the body that you feel needs strengthening or healing. As you lay them on any part of your body, think of an image from **nature**, perhaps like the body of water in the image above.

5. Keep your hands there until, eventually you feel the **energy** enter the body and start to travel into other adjacent parts of the body.

6. Once you have finished, sit and relax, perhaps with your arms crossed and hands on opposite shoulders, **breathing** slowly and deeply. And enjoy the experience of basking in the energy for 5 to 6 minutes.

Going with the flow, Tai Chi & Energy

As a practicing Christian, I learnt a lot from the plight of Jesus Christ through the world. The important lessons to learn are many. One stands out for me. Jesus kept moving forward as he made his walk with the cross to be put to death. He did not complain and knew this was what was to happen in order to ascend to a level nobody could dream off.

When moving from A to B, just keep moving forward, whether you are in a place of positivity or negativity. Nobody has lived a completely positive life in the way which we believe it to be in an ideal movie. Positivity is by far a better **vibrational** compliment for creating abundance in your life, but if you cannot remain this way, then move forward in any case.... with tears in your eyes and heaviness in your heart....one step at a time.

But remember not to waste your energy unnecessarily. What do I mean? Energy can be unnecessarily depleted in so many different ways. Unnecessary tension in your muscles can drain your energies and so too can unengaged muscles. Unengaged muscles around the spine can cause it to crumble and the energy within your brain eventually fizzles out. Never waste your energy by keeping too much physical tension or relaxing areas of the body that are supposed to be tense, like the spine. In the world of Tai Chi, slow movement is known to amass **power** and true strength. Take a slow long look at each muscle group in your body and ask yourself whether it is **beneficial** being tense or relaxed. The philosophy behind the **symbol** YinYang teaches us this very principle over and over on so many different levels.

The philosophy of embracing the **good** the bad and the ugly can be applied to many different dimensions, that is, in one energy type you find the opposite. There is no real **good** or bad energy, it just does different things to the body. The scientific world will verify that energy is just turned into different forms. Within strength, there is weakness, an Achilles heel perhaps. But that same weakness can quite easily turn into strength further down the stream of time. There is always a pivotal point. It is at this turning point in which one energy type gets converted into its very opposite.

In Tai Chi or any slow **meditative** movement, you understand power comes with gentleness and there is awesome power in yielding. Yielding helps a Tai ji master to redirect the energy of an assailant and use it against them.

The mind can also channel a specific intent and the body when in a highly **relaxed** state becomes to be receptive to the thought pattern created by the mind. Be focused and alert enough to create a specific type of intent in all that you do and you will invariably create powerful levels of energy within yourself for **healing** and zestful appetite for life.

A true **master** will couple all the soft and slow movement he or she performs with hidden **strength**. You should feel so engaged with everything including the Earth itself that your physical and mental energy partially sink into it. This sinking process will allow you to tap into the **energies** residing in the very earth itself and **syphon** them into your body. You can also create the same effect from many still **meditation** modalities if you employ the same technique. Keep every Tai hi movement slow and graceful always but infuse it with subtle power. Move softly and be free flowing like a calm wind. Training this way in the Tai Chi Chaun will enable one to learn how to apply this dynamic to life itself.

I sincerely wish you many blessings in all aspects of your life but remember the sole purpose of this book is to create happiness yourself through meditation. NOBODY in history became great without putting in work of some kind. For me, this means plenty of **internal and external work**. I see meditation as a tool to upgrade the human state in the process of our evolution. It can enhance your performance and create more presence and the interaction with everything and everyone becomes more meaningful. The process of life becomes more fulfilling and interesting. It helps us to flush away any mental detritus that scatters our energy in different directions. With less distractions we can easily find what we are truly passionate about and what gives us the energy to move in the direction guided by our higher self.

I trust that you will revisit the meditations and passages in this book routinely. I wish you many blessings in all dimensions of your life.

With very best wishes to all,

Paul Tavares

25449124R00061

Printed in Great Britain
by Amazon